AMERICAN BATTLESHIPS: A Complet

By: Arthur C. Unger

ACR 1 USS MAINE - the sinking of the Maine in Cuba was erroneously blamed on Spain precipitating the 1898 Spanish American War.

BB39 USS ARIZONA - the sinking of the Arizona in the 1941 Japanese sneak attack on Pearl Harbor became America's rallying cry for WWII.

This is a chronology of battleships, majestic giants that once roamed the oceans of the world, demonstrating a nation's naval power. It is a study of the ships that bore the distinction of being a Battleship of the United States Navy. Every hull number is accounted for and the role that each battleship played in the story is told. It begins with the Second Class Battleships Texas and Maine and ends with the Iowa Class, which helped the United States win World War II. The Iowas gave 50 years of glorious service, serving in WWII, Korea, Vietnam, and Desert Storm. Eight battleships remain, now serving our Country as War Memorials. This is their story, from the Era of the Dreadnoughts to the present day.

Fully illustrated with 92 pictures, including pictures of every United States Navy battleship that ever was or might have been.

AMERICAN BATTLESHIPS: A Complete Chronology

By: Arthur C. Unger

Custer1876 Publications

Wilmington, North Carolina

2017

Copyright c 2016, 2017
By: Arthur C. Unger

Library of Congress Catalog Number - 02016904389

ISBN NUMBER 978-0-692-67084-2

PRINTINGS 2016, 2017

CUSTER1876 PUBLICATIONS

WILMINGTON, NORTH CAROLINA

Dedicated to my wonderful wife and proof reader Grace.
Thank you for being you!

PREFACE

For more than fifty years, a country's naval might was measured by the number of Capital Ships it possessed and no Capital Ship was more valued than a battleship. A country's maritime prestige was measured by a sole parameter, the number of battleships in its navy. Many countries devoted huge portions of their national defense budgets to the building of one or two of these sea going behemoths. In their early days a battleship was of the size and displacement of a modern destroyer, approximately 6,000 tons and within the brief period of but fifty years evolved into immense gargantuans displacing 80,000 to 90,000 tons when fully armed and manned. Then, when at their zenith for speed, size, and armament, they became obsolete and very soon thereafter extinct, much like the dinosaurs.

Even today if one were to ask a citizen of a country with an impressive naval history, to name a great ship in their country's past, you would hear names like Hood, Bismarck, Prince of Wales, Yamato, Arizona, and Iowa. Though without a doubt it was the aircraft carriers that were decisive and carried the day in World War II, it is the battleships that are far better remembered. The memories that are stirred when these great names are mentioned create images of awesome monsters slugging it out, much like heavy weight boxers, toe to toe and eye to eye. They were capable, even before the advent of radar, of hurling 2500 pound projectiles at targets as far as twenty miles away, with as much deadly accuracy as a modern laser guided missile.

These vessels of majesty and destiny inspired hundreds of books and movies, recalling the great confrontations, acts of power, devastation, and horrific loss of life, which was embedded in the history of the dreadnoughts. Dreadnought was a generic term for battleship. It was derived from the HMS Dreadnought launched in 1906, by the British Navy, and was the first all big gun battleship. This set in motion the great naval arms race that was to ensue for the next forty years.

The mere mention of the Hood or Arizona, creates mental images of unparalleled destruction, huge ships totally destroyed by a single direct hit, with near complete loss of life. The Bismarck was a ship that could not be sunk, no matter how many direct hits the British inflicted upon her. The Bismarck finally succumbed to a massive torpedo attack, against its lesser protected lower hull, below the water line. The Nevada was the only battleship to fire its boilers and make steam at Pearl Harbor. It lived to survive the atomic bomb tests Able and Baker at Bikini Atoll, refusing to accept its destiny until it was felled by naval gunfire superior to its armament.

Of all the great Naval Powers, no nation ever achieved more success with their battleships, than the United States did. While the United States did not build the biggest of the battleships, it certainly built the best and manned them with superior crews. With the advent of radar, the United States Navy became the master of night time gunnery action. The United States is the only naval power of the Dreadnought Era to have never lost a battleship to the fire of an enemy battleship. What follows is a brief history and chronology of The American Navy's Battleships.

CONTENTS

THE FAST BATTLESHIPS OF WORLD WAR II 126

THE INTENDED THAT NEVER WERE 138

THE GREAT WHITE FLEET

In late 1907, United States President Theodore "Teddy" Roosevelt decided to demonstrate to the world that the United States had come of age as an international naval power. To accomplish this feat, he committed sixteen of his new fleet of battleships, seven destroyers (Arethusa, a tender, Hopkins, Hull, Lawrence, Stewart, Truxton, and Whipple), and five fleet auxiliary ships (Culgoa, a store ship, Glacier, a store ship, Panther, a repair ship, Relief, a hospital ship, and Yankton, a tender) to circumnavigate the globe. All the ships were painted white, which was the Navy's peacetime color, sported gilt trim, and had red, white, and blue banners on their bows. The fleet was commanded by Rear Admiral Robley D. Evans, when it departed Hampton Roads, Virginia. Unfortunately, due Admiral Evans poor health, he was unable to continue on in command. Rear Admiral Charles S. Sperry was given command of the fleet, on its departure from San Francisco, California, and the Division Commands were reorganized as well.

When the fleet initially departed Hampton Roads, Virginia, the two Kearsarge Class ships, BB5 Kearsarge and BB6 Kentucky were already deemed too old and unfit for battle, but they could and did add to the demonstration of naval power. The original composition of the fleet included BB8 Alabama and BB10 Maine. However, when the fleet reached San Francisco, they were detached due to mechanical trouble and replaced by BB9 Wisconsin and BB14 Nebraska. BB8 Alabama and BB10 Maine were repaired and continued on for separate circumnavigation of the globe. Their itinerary included Honolulu, Guam, Manila, Singapore, Colombo, Suez, Naples, Gibraltar, and the Azores, returning home on October 20, 1908. Although the fleet never contained more than sixteen battleships at one time, eighteen battleships participated, at least partially, in the voyage. The fleet was divided into two Squadrons, of two divisions each, with commanders shown as the fleet departed from San Francisco, California:

- The First Squadron, First Division, commanded by Rear Admiral Charles S. Sperry, consisted of four ships of the 1906 Connecticut Class:

    o BB18 Connecticut – the Fleet, Squadron, and Division Flagship

    o BB20 Vermont

    o BB21 Kansas

    o BB22 Minnesota

- The First Squadron, Second Division, commanded by Rear Admiral Richard Wainwright, consisted of four ships of the 1904 Virginia Class:

    o BB13 Virginia

    o BB15 Georgia – the Division Flagship

    o BB16 New Jersey

    o BB17 Rhode Island

- The Second Squadron, Third Division, commanded by Rear Admiral William H. Emory, contained one ship of the 1906 Connecticut Class and three ships of the 1902 Maine Class:

    o BB11 Missouri

    o BB12 Ohio

- o BB14 Nebraska

- o BB19 Louisiana – the Squadron and Division Flagship

- The Second Squadron, Fourth Division, commanded by Rear Admiral Seaton Schroeder, contained two ships of the 1901 Illinois Class and two ships of the 1900 Kearsarge Class:

  - o BB 5 Kearsarge

  - o BB 6 Kentucky

  - o BB 7 Illinois

  - o BB 9 Wisconsin – the Division Flagship

1: THE GREAT WHITE FLEET AT SEA WITH THE FLAGSHIP BB18 CONNECTICUT LEADING

The Fleet departed from Hampton Roads, Virginia, on December 16, 1907 and returned some fourteen months later on February 22, 1909. The ports of call during the odyssey were:

- Port of Spain, Trinidad
- Rio de Janeiro, Brazil
- Punta Arenas, Chile
- Callao, Peru
- Magdalena Bay, Mexico
- San Francisco, California
- Puget Sound, Washington and back to San Francisco, California
- Honolulu, Hawaii
- Auckland, New Zealand
- Sydney, Australia
- Melbourne, Australia
- Albany, Australia
- Manila, Philippines
- Yokohama, Japan
- Amoy, China
- Colombo, Ceylon
- Suez, Egypt
- Naples, Italy
- Gibraltar
- And returning to Hampton Roads, Virginia

This fleet manned by approximately 14,000 officers and men covered approximately 43,000 nautical miles, proudly displaying the American Flag and the United States' newly developed naval power.   Subsequent to this voyage, the United States was regarded worldwide as a first class naval power.

JUTLAND THE GRAND MOMENT FOR BATTLESHIPS

On December 11, 1906, the British Navy commissioned the HMS Dreadnought and the race towards Naval Armageddon began. This was an advance in naval warfare so astoundingly immense that no other naval power, large or small, could ignore it. HMS Dreadnought was the first all big gun battleship. She displaced 18,120 tons, had ten 12" guns as main armament, carrying 80 rounds per gun in her magazines, twenty seven 3" guns as secondary armament, could achieve a speed of 21 knots and had a range of 6,600 nautical miles. She had two and a half times the fire power and was 25% faster than any other battleship then afloat. She raised the bar of naval warfare to a new standard by making all existing battleships worldwide obsolete.

2: HMS DREADNOGHT CIRCA 1907

Navies worldwide then commenced their individual version of imitation is the sincerest form of flattery, by designing and building their own version of a dreadnought.

16

The race expanded exponentially as each country built more and more dreadnought type battleships, with every new class far more deadly than its predecessors.

The Battle of Jutland, fought in the North Sea during World War I, between the Royal Navy's Grand Fleet commanded by Admiral John Jellicoe and the Imperial German Navy's High Seas Fleet commanded by Vice-Admiral Reinhard Scheer from May 31 to June 1, 1916, was history's single largest clash of huge fleets led by battleships.

The British had a vast numerical superiority with its fleet having 151 combat vessels consisting of 28 battleships, 9 battlecruisers, 8 armored cruisers, 26 light cruisers, 78 destroyers, 1 minelayer, and 1 seaplane carrier. The numerically inferior German fleet included 99 combat vessels consisting of 16 battleships, 5 battlecruisers, 6 pre-dreadnoughts, 11 light cruisers and 61 torpedo boats. When looking at the material available to both sides, one would expect the numerically superior British Fleet to achieve a major victory over the vastly inferior German fleet.

The Germans, however, sustained far smaller losses in material and manpower, losing 1 battlecruiser, 1 pre-dreadnought, 4 light cruisers and 5 torpedo boats, 62,300 total tons sunk, with 2,551 killed in action. The British lost 3 battlecruisers, 3 armored cruisers, and 8 destroyers, 113,300 total tons sunk, with 6,094 killed in action. Numbers, however, do not always tell the tale. While the Germans achieved a material victory based upon ships sunk, the British achieved a tactical victory in that the German fleet returned to port, never to venture out to sea again for the duration of the War.

The naval engagement was the largest single concentration of battleships, 44 being the combined total of the two fleets, and produced a non-result with most considering the battle a draw. The Germans dismally failed to achieve their objective of destroying a substantial portion of the British Fleet. There were no confrontations between battleships, no engagements with battleships exchanging broadsides; the actual fighting was between the smaller vessels, with an edge in material destroyed going to the Germans.

Neither before nor after Jutland was there ever a confrontation of two fleets containing so many battleships. While Jutland may have been the high water mark of the dreadnought/battleship era, it was a non-event when it came to actual engagements between battleships. Actual engagements between battleships, when they did occur, involved far fewer numbers of battleships divided among the combatants.

WASHINGTON NAVAL TREATY OF 1923

Subsequent to World War I and the carnage and devastation it inflicted upon the world, the five major victorious naval powers of the world, England, France, Italy, Japan, and the United States, met between November, 1921 and February, 1922 in what was known as the Washington Naval Conference. The purpose of the conference was to produce a treaty that would prevent a naval arms race, similar to the one that preceded World War I, from ever again occurring.

The intent was to achieve this objective by limiting the construction of capital ships, battleships, battlecruisers, and aircraft carriers, by limiting the number of capital ships each country could maintain in its respective fleets and restricting total tonnage. While it did not limit the number of lesser class vessels, they were limited in size by being restricted to no more than 10,000 tons displacement.

When the treaty was finally negotiated and agreed to, it limited the total tonnage each party could have of capital ships with a ratio of 5: 5: 3: 1.75: 1.75, respectively, for England, the United States, Japan, France, and Italy. What this translated to in actual tonnage for Capital Ships (battleships and battlecruisers) was 525,000: 525,000: 315,000: 175,000: 175,000 and additionally for aircraft carriers was 135,000: 135,000: 81,000: 60,000: 60,000, again respectively, for England, the United States, Japan, France, and Italy. The treaty further limited the size of any individual battleship or battlecruiser to 35,000 tons and prohibited their having any guns larger than a sixteen inch caliber.

Aircraft carriers were limited to 27,000 tons and could not carry more than ten large guns, which could not have a caliber greater than eight inches. A permitted exception allowed each participant to use the hulls of two existing capital ships by converting them into aircraft carriers of no more than 33,000 tons each.

At the time the treaty went into effect the United States was in the process of constructing the South Dakota Class of Battleships, from which six ships were intended, all of which were in varying stages of construction but none were complete. All six, BB49 South Dakota, BB50 Indiana, BB51 Montana, BB52 North Carolina, BB53 Iowa, and BB54 Massachusetts were scrapped pursuant to the treaty.

3: SCRAPPING OF LARGE CALIBER GUNS LEFT FOREGROUND; AND DISMANTLING OF THE SOUTH CAROLINA BB26 RIGHT BACKGROUND, PURSUANT TO THE WASHINGTON NAVAL TREAY OF 1923

An accord was finally achieved and a treaty produced on February 6, 1922, which was then ratified by the signatories on August 17, 1923. This treaty was modified by the London Naval Treaty of 1930 and the Second London Naval Treaty of 1936. While these treaties were well intended and did produce an approximate ten year hiatus in the construction of capital ships, the wheels came off the wagon in the mid 1930's. Japan, and Italy renounced the treaties, while Germany ignored the treaty's existence, and all three countries began construction of new Capital Ships beyond treaty limitations. France, England, and the United States retaliated by beginning their own new construction beyond treaty limits. A new naval arms race ensued, leading the entire world down the path to the Armageddon to be known as World War II. The first major escalating blow was delivered by Japan when it ordered two battleships from the Super Battleship Class Yamato. In March, 1937, the Yamato was ordered, followed by the Musashi in June, 1937. These monsters displaced 72,800 tons, had a main armament of nine 18 inch guns, a secondary armament of six 6 inch guns, an armor belt of 16 inches, speed of 27 knots, cruising range of 7,200 nautical miles, and were manned by a crew of approximately 2,700 officers and men.

The Yamato and Musashi were a totally new level of battleship, as they displaced more than twice the 35,000 tons allowed by the Treaties, had a primary armament of 18 inch guns, far larger than the 16 inches allowed by treaty, belt armor of 16 inches, and a speed of 27 knots. What this meant was they were larger, faster, better armed, and better armored than any ship in any other country's fleet. The best that the United States had at this time was the Colorado Class, consisting of BB45 Colorado, BB46 Maryland and BB48 West Virginia. The Colorado Class, displaced 31,500 tons, had eight 16 inch guns, 16 inch armor, and a speed of 21 knots. In layman terms they were half the size, slower, weaker, and inadequately armored when compared to the Yamato Class. The guiding concept behind the thickness of armor in battleships was 16 inches of armor could withstand a hit from a projectile fired by a 16 inch gun. In essence, the Yamato Class, were they to engage in a surface battle with existing United States battleships, would in all likelihood annihilate its opposition and remain basically unscathed.

The United States realized that a new naval race had commenced and that it would be unable to counteract Japan's Navy in the Pacific with its now obsolete fleet, if it stood idly by. Accordingly, on August 1, 1937 the two ships of the North Carolina Class were ordered, displacing 44,800 tons, having nine 16 inch guns, armor ranging from 12 to 16 inches and a speed of 27 knots. On December 15, 1938, four ships of the South Dakota Class were ordered. This class would displace 44,500 tons, have nine 16 inch guns, armor ranging from 12 to 18 inches and a speed of 27 knots. The next ratchet up was on July 1, 1939 when six ships for the Iowa Class were ordered. These would displace 57,000 tons, have nine 16 inch guns, armor ranging from 12 to 19 inches and a speed of 35 knots. The final gauntlet to be added to the naval arms race, by the United States, was the five ships of the Montana Class, ordered January 1, 1941. They were planned to displace 71,000 tons, have a main armament of twelve 16 inch guns, armor ranging from 16 to 22 inches and a speed of 28 knots. On July 21, 1943, the order for the Montana Class was canceled. The United States had realized that it was on track to winning the war and the Montanas would be unnecessary and were obsolete, before they were ever built.

Other countries now also joined the race. On July 29, 1936, England ordered five ships of the King George V Class which displaced 43,000 tons, and had ten 14 inch guns, 14.7 inch armor, and a speed of 28 knots. On July 1, 1936, Germany ordered two ships of the Bismarck Class which displaced 50,300 tons, and had eight 15 inch guns, 12 to 14 inch armor, and a speed of 30 knots. On June 10, 1934, Italy ordered four ships of the Littorio Class which displaced 45,200 tons, and had nine 15 inch guns, 11 to 14 inch armor, and a speed of 30 knots. On October 22, 1935, France ordered four ships of the Richelieu Class which displaced 49,000 tons, and had eight 15 inch guns, 13 to 17 inch armor, and a speed 30 knots. While the race to Naval Armageddon was now well underway, little did the participants realize at the time, that race was futile as the battleships' day had come and gone during the hiatus caused by the various treaties.

No longer would naval engagements be won or lost by huge fleets, in sight of each other, firing highly destructive projectiles from large guns. Fleets would now engage, hundreds of miles apart, by launching large numbers of aircraft armed with aerial bombs and torpedoes, to determine the outcome of the battle. A classic example of this new form of naval warfare was the Battle of Midway, fought June, 1942 between Japan and the United States. The opposing fleets were hundreds of miles apart, Japan lost all four of its carriers, while the United States lost only one of its three carriers in the engagement.

Much as the dinosaurs were replaced as the dominant species by mammals; battleships were to be replaced by aircraft carriers and their airplanes as the dominant naval warship.

23

THE BEGINNING OF THE END OF THE BATTLESHIP ERA

TARANTO AND SALAMIS

The naval Battle of Taranto occurred on November 11 and 12, 1940, between forces of the British and Italian navies. The British utilized naval aviation to devastate several Italian vessels, including three battleships. The attack was made by obsolete swordfish bi-planes, launched from the carrier HMS Illustrious, in two waves, with twelve swordfish in the first wave followed by nine in the second. Half of the strike force was armed with torpedoes, the balance with aerial bombs. Three Italian battleships were severely damaged: the Conte di Cavour was sunk and subsequently raised but never fully repaired, Caio Duillo was saved by being run aground, and Littorio was hit by three torpedoes and also had to be run aground. The Littorio and Caio Duillo were subsequently repaired and returned to service.

This battle was the precursor of Pearl Harbor. The actions of the British and the results they obtained by utilizing aircraft armed with torpedoes in shallow waters, were well noted by Japanese Navy and ignored by the American Navy. The interest and lack of interest displayed by the Japanese and American navies, respectively, contributed greatly to the carnage that took place during the 1941 Japanese attack on Pearl Harbor.

In 1914, the United States sold BB23 Mississippi and BB24 Idaho to Greece. They were renamed Kilkis and Lemnos respectively. On April 10, 1941, Kilkis and Lemnos were moored in the harbor of Salamis, and sunk by German dive bombers (see images 50 and 51 on page 98).

4: TARANTO HARBOR CIRCA 1930

5: A SWORDFISH TORPEDO BOMBER OF THE TYPE USED BY THE BRITISH DURING THE BATTLE OF

TARANTO AND THE ATTACK ON THE BISMARCK

25

PEARL HARBOR

The Japanese attack on Pearl Harbor, December 7, 1941, though it caused horrific loss of life and extensive damage to the eight United States battleships∗ moored in the harbor, it failed to deliver the knockout blow Japan had hoped for. The Arizona was the victim of an aerial bomb that hit near the forward magazine causing the ship to explode and immediately sink. Of the 1512 crew men on board, 1177 perished with their ship. The Oklahoma sustained nine torpedo hits, causing it to capsize. Of her officers and men on board, 429 were killed in the attack, with approximately 290 crew men being trapped inside her when she capsized. Valiant attempts were made to save those entombed in the ship, but in the end they failed with only 32 being rescued. The Oklahoma was eventually raised, but could not be repaired prior to the war's end. She was sold for scrap and sank in a storm, while being towed to California to succumb to her fate of being scrapped. The sinking provided a nobler end for this proud vessel, than the intended cutter's torch. The attack failed to eliminate the ability of the United States Navy to oppose the Japanese in the Pacific theater. Japan would not achieve the victory in a quick war that it hoped for and wound up losing a prolonged war which it had feared.

∗ An easy way to remember these eight battleships is with the words CAMP TOWN, which uses the first initial of each battleship's name – California BB44, Arizona BB39, Maryland BB46, Pennsylvania BB38 -- and   --   Tennessee BB43, Oklahoma BB37, West Virginia BB48, Nevada BB36

6: BATTLESHIP ROW AT INCEPTION OF THE ATTACK

7: PEARL HARBOR A PICTURE TAKEN FROM AN ATTACKING JAPANESE AIRCRAFT

8: AERIAL VIEW OF "BATTLESHIP ROW" MOORINGS AT FORD ISLAND PEARL HARBOR, THREE DAYS AFTER THE ATTACK. IN THE UPPER LEFT IS THE USS CALIFORNIA BB-44 SUNK, WITH SMALLER VESSELS BY HER. FROM THE CALIFORNIA GOING LEFT TO RIGHT ARE: USS MARYLAND BB-46, LIGHTLY DAMAGED, THE CAPSIZED USS OKLAHOMA BB-37 OUTBOARD, USS TENNESSEE (BB-43), LIGHTLY DAMAGED, WITH THE SUNK USS WEST VIRGINIA (BB-48) OUTBOARD, AND FINALLY THE USS ARIZONA BB-39 SUNK.

PRINCE OF WALES, HOOD AND BISMARCK – BATTLE OF THE DENMARK STRAIT

The Battle of the Denmark Strait occurred on May 24, 1941, between elements of the British Royal Navy and the German Kriegsmarine. The British held a numerical superiority of four vessels to two; however, the main combatants were essentially equal. The British had one battleship, the Prince of Wales, and one battlecruiser, the Hood, which the Germans opposed with one battleship, the Bismarck and one heavy cruiser, the Prinz Eugen.

The Prince of Wales, a King George V class battleship, displaced 43,800 tons, had 14.7 inch armor and boasted ten 14 inch guns in two turrets of two each, superimposed on two turrets of three each. The Hood displaced 42,700 tons, had armor ranging from 6 to 12 inches, and had eight 15 inch guns in four turrets of two each.

9: HMS HOOD CIRCA 1924

10: HMS PRINCE OF WALES 1941

They were opposed by the Bismarck displacing 50,300, having 12.6 inches of armor, and eight 15 inch guns in four turrets of two each. The Prinz Eugen displaced 18,700 tons, had 3 inch armor, and carried eight 8 inch guns in four twin turrets.

11: BISMARCK 1941

30

12: PRINZ EUGEN

This battle was over virtually before it started. The Hood fired first, the Bismarck returned fire and ten minutes after the firing began a shell from the Bismarck struck the Hood near the aft magazines and the Hood immediately exploded, killing all but three of her crew of nearly 1400. The Prince of Wales and Bismarck continued to exchange fire, with the Prince of Wales sustaining damage to its main armament, causing her to break off the engagement. The Bismarck meanwhile sustained damage to its forward fuel tanks, forcing it to abandon its attempt to break out into the Atlantic, and forcing her to return to port for repairs. A tactical victory was attributed to the Germans.

The British then commenced an all-out effort to find and destroy the Bismarck, committing among other vessels, the aircraft carrier Ark Royal and the battleships Rodney, a 1920's vintage battleship, and King George V, a modern battleship of the same class as Prince of Wales, to the hunt.

13: HMS RODNEY 1942

14: HMS ARK ROYAL CIRCA 1939

On May 26, 1941, Bismarck was attacked, by Swordfish torpedo bombers (see image 5 on page 25) from the carrier Ark Royal. These were the same type of puny bi-planes that inflicted the damage on the Italian battleships at Taranto. The British got lucky and one of the torpedoes jammed the Bismarck's rudder in a turning position preventing her escape to a German held port in France. The Bismarck could barely make 10 knots and was steering towards the British and not safety in France.

On May 27, 1941, the British surface vessels caught up with Bismarck and a battle of nearly two hours ensued. The Bismarck was essentially helpless, being unable to maintain a battle speed and could neither steer nor maneuver. She eventually sank due to shellfire, torpedo hits and scuttling. Only 111 of her crew of nearly 2200 survived.

The Bismarck was brought to her knees by a torpedo dropped from an obsolete bi-plane, which prior to the war was thought as likely to occur as an elephant being dropped from a mosquito bite. This was another in a growing list of nails in the coffin of the concept that battleships were the main Capital Ship in a country's navy.

THE REPULSE AND THE PRINCE OF WALES – NAVAL BATTLE OFF MALAYA

A mere three days after the American debacle at Pearl Harbor, the British suffered a far less well known but nearly equal naval fiasco of their own. Officially it was named the Naval Battle off Malaya.

The British government had decided to send a relief fleet to aid in the defense of Singapore; it was named Force, commanded by Vice-Admiral Sir Tom Philips. Admiral Philips was known, probably behind his back, as "Tom Thumb" due to his being only five feet four inches tall. Philips possessed two of the worst possible personality traits, for a military commander, that being he was opinionated and incorrect. He was convinced that:

- The Royal Air Force could not protect his fleet because the only aircraft available were antiquated Brewster Buffalo fighters

- He believed that Japanese planes could not operate so far from land

- Like most of the old school Naval Officers, he felt his ships were relatively safe from severe damage by an air attack

- He was unaware of the quality of Japanese medium range bombers

- He underestimated the fighting prowess of the Japanese.

Force Z consisted of the modern battleship Prince of Wales, the World War I vintage battlecruiser Repulse, and four destroyers Electra, Express, Vampire and Malaya. At 5 pm, on December 8, 1941, Philips ordered Force Z to depart Singapore, in the hope of intercepting and destroying a convoy believed to be near Kota Bharu. On December 9, Force Z was spotted by two Japanese reconnaissance airplanes and the Japanese

Submarine I-65, while the British destroyer Tenedos was detached and returned to Singapore due to low fuel.

At 11:40 am on December 10, Force Z was attacked by 17 torpedo bombers, one scoring a crippling blow on the Prince of Wales. At 12:20 a second group of bombers attacked, registering three more hits on the Prince of Wales. Repulse suffered at least four torpedo hits and at 12:33 pm Repulse sank. At 12:41 pm Prince of Wales was subjected to a high altitude bombardment and at 1:18 pm she too sank. The Japanese lost a total of three aircraft during the entire engagement. In roughly one hour and forty minutes the British lost a modern battleship and a World War I vintage battlecruiser, compared to Japanese losses of three aircraft.

Thus, as 1941 drew to an end, the era of the Battleship being the Queen of the Fleet was ending as well. The four battles previously discussed, Taranto, the Denmark Strait, Pearl Harbor, and the Naval Battle off Malaya, ended the myth that battleships were invulnerable to attacks by aircraft and proved the exact opposite. The then, new, prevailing view was that aircraft armed with torpedoes and aerial bombs were the main attack weapon in a navy's arsenal.

1942 brought a new era to naval warfare. Carriers were the lynch-pins of the Fleets and battleships were relegated to shore bombardments and being floating anti-aircraft platforms to defend carriers. Henceforth when fleets would engage each other, they would be separated by great distances, never actually visualizing the enemy, and fighting with the new form of naval artillery – aircraft attacking with aerial bombs and torpedoes.

THE LAST HURRAH FOR BATTLESHIPS

After General Douglas MacArthur's forces successfully landed in the Philippines, from Leyte Gulf, the Japanese Navy decided to make a total effort to drive the American land forces into the sea and destroy the U.S. Navy's fleet supporting the landing.

The Japanese divided the naval forces committed to this counterattack into three groups:

The Northern Force, commanded by Vice Admiral Ozawa, consisted of four aircraft carriers which had very few airplanes. The purpose of the Northern Force was to be the bait that would lure the American carriers away from Leyte Gulf. This group included the Zuikaku (the last surviving carrier of the six carriers that attacked Pearl Harbor), Zuiho, Chitose, and Chiyoda, two old battleships Hyuga and Ise (both of which were modified by the removal of their aft turrets and had the aft portion of the ships turned into mini-carriers), three light cruisers and nine destroyers. There were 108 aircraft dispersed among the four carriers while the old converted battleships carried no aircraft.

The Center Force, commanded by Vice Admiral Kurita, would attack by going through the San Bernardino Strait into the Philippine Sea. The Center Force was the most powerful of the three Forces. This group contained five battleships including the two super battleships Yamato and Musashi (these were the two largest battleships ever built displacing nearly 72,000 tons, having three turrets of three 18 inch guns and a secondary armament of two turrets of three six inch guns), plus the Haruna, Kongo, and Nagato.   Completing the group were ten heavy cruisers, two light cruisers and fifteen destroyers.

15: YAMATO AT SEA CIRCA 1941

The Southern Force, commanded by Vice-Admirals Nishimura and Shima, were to attack by entering Leyte Gulf through the Surigao Strait.   The Southern Force contained two old battleships Yamashiro and Fuso, one heavy cruiser and four destroyers.

There were minor clashes on October 22 and 23, 1944, with the American submarines Darter and Dace attacking Kurita's Center Force, as it moved through Palawan Passage. Darter scored four torpedo hits on the heavy cruiser Atago, and two torpedo hits on the heavy cruiser Takao, while Dace scored four hits on the heavy cruiser Maya. Atago and Maya sank almost immediately, while Takao limped back to Brunei escorted by two destroyers.   Round one was a lopsided American victory.   Round two would be in the Sibuyan Sea.

BATTLE OF THE SIBUYAN SEA

The Battle of the Sibuyan Sea occurred on October 24, 1944. Aircraft from the American carriers attacked Kurita's Center Force scoring aerial bomb hits on the battleships Musashi, Yamato, and Nagato, while severely damaging the heavy cruiser Myoko.

16: THE YAMATO UNDER ATTACK IN THE SIBYUAN SEA

A second wave of aircraft from Essex, Intrepid and Lexington scored ten more hits on Musashi, which withdrew listing to port. A third wave from Enterprise and Franklin scored eleven more hits with bombs and eight with torpedoes. Kurita withdrew his fleet, passing the devastated Musashi as he departed. Musashi capsized and sank approximately 5 pm.

17: BATTLESHIP MUSASHI UNDER ATTACK IN THE SIBUYAN SEA.

At the battle's end the tally was Japan losing Musashi and having the light cruiser Myoko devastated, while the Americans lost the light carrier USS Princeton. Round two goes to the Americans.   Next round will occur in the Surigao Strait.

BATTLE OF SURIGAO STRAIT

On October 25, 1944 the Japanese Southern Force, in two groups, proceeded into Surigao Strait. Vice Admiral Shima commanding two heavy cruisers, one light cruiser, and four destroyers, while Vice Admiral Nishimura commanded two old battleships Yamashiro and Fuso, one heavy cruiser and four destroyers. The opening salvo was a major torpedo onslaught from American PT Boats and Destroyers laying in ambush for the Japanese. Waiting for the Japanese to pass through the gauntlet of torpedoes was the bulk of the American fleet, under the command of Rear Admiral Jesse B. Oldendorf. The fleet included, six battleships (West Virginia BB48, Maryland BB46, Mississippi BB41, Tennessee BB43, California BB44 and Pennsylvania BB38, all but the Mississippi BB41 were victims of the Japanese attack on Pearl Harbor), four heavy cruisers, four light cruisers, 28 destroyers and 39 PT boats.

The carnage began at 3:00 am, Fuso was struck by torpedoes and sank, Yamashiro, though hit by torpedoes, continued forward. Two of the four destroyers were sunk and a third hit (it retreated but later sank). The West Virginia BB48, California BB44, and Tennessee BB43, by utilizing their radar, were able to fire on the Japanese well before the Japanese could return fire. The three American battleships, respectively fired 93 sixteen inch shells, 63 fourteen inch shells and 69 fourteen inch shells, at the Japanese. The Maryland BB46 added 48 sixteen inch shells to the salvos, while the Pennsylvania BB38 could not locate the target and did not fire at all. The Mississippi BB41, which was last in the battle line, only fired one broadside but it was an historic one.

40

It was the last time one battleship fired upon another battleship, thus officially ending the "battleship era". The Yamashiro sank at 4:20 am. The five old battleships, West Virginia BB48, California BB44, Tennessee BB43, Maryland BB46, and Pennsylvania BB38, who were victims of the dastardly attack on Pearl Harbor and had been raised from the carnage, repaired and refitted, finally achieved revenge for the attack on Pearl Harbor in the Battle of Suriago Strait. Round three went decisively to the Americans.

When all the losses were tallied, American Naval Forces scored a decisive victory over Japan. Japan's losses were one super battleship, two old battleships, three light cruisers, one fleet carrier and approximately 12,500 killed in action, while America lost one light carrier, 2 escort carriers, 2 destroyers and had approximately 3,000 casualties.

BATTLE OF OKINAWA

In April, 1945, the Yamato, the last of Japan's two super battleships (her sister ship Musashi having been sunk during the Battle of Leyte Gulf), was given a Kamikaze-like assignment. She was ordered to proceed to Okinawa, run herself aground, and fight defending the island until she was destroyed. On April 7, 1945, while steaming towards Okinawa, the Yamato was sighted by American submarines. At 12:30 pm the Americans commenced an attack against the Yamato with 280 carrier based bomber and torpedo aircraft. The Yamato suffered five bomb hits which caused a great deal of damage. At 12:45 pm the Yamato was struck by a torpedo on her port side. Shortly thereafter, the Yamato was struck again by two or three torpedoes (the third hit is unconfirmed) on her port side. A second wave struck at 1:00 pm, this was a coordinated effort of high altitude dive bombers and torpedo planes. Yamato suffered three more torpedo hits on her port side and one on her starboard side. Yamato began to list severely to port and became unable to fire her main armament. The last and third wave struck at 1:40 pm scoring at least four bomb hits and four more torpedo hits three to the port side and one starboard. At 2:02 pm Yamato's crew received the order to abandon ship. At 2:20 pm Yamato lost power, capsized, one of her forward magazines exploded and she sank rapidly. Effectively, Japan no longer had a surface fleet of any consequence.

18: THE YAMATO EXPLODES JUST PRIOR TO SINKING.

THE FAILURES OF AMERICA AND JAPAN AT PEARL HARBOR

THE MISTAKES MADE BY UNITED STATES

The United States committed several major blunders at Pearl Harbor, which either caused or contributed to the day's carnage, which initially made it appear that Japan had won a great victory.   Notable among these errors were:

- Failing to pay note to and learn from the Battle of Taranto. Thereby, not taking the necessary precautions to prevent a similar disaster from occurring at Pearl Harbor

- Not having torpedo nets in place to protect ships moored in the harbor

- Ignoring the early warnings received from the surface vessels USS Antares and USS Ward that an attack was underway

- Failing to follow up on the detection of inbound aircraft, by the Army personnel manning the Opana Point radar installation, on Oahu's north shore.

- The failure to have a long range air reconnaissance plan, that utilized scout aircraft, to observe an early warning defense perimeter around Oahu

- General Short's obsessive fear that Native Japanese living on Oahu would commit acts of sabotage. This caused him to order that land base aircraft be parked together in groups, thereby rendering them highly vulnerable to an air attack

- Failure to have defensive aircraft on alert and at the ready, and or airborne

44

- The incompetent and almost non-existent efforts by the U.S. War Department, in Washington D.C., to keep Admiral Kimmel and General Short apprised that war with Japan was imminent

Taranto should have demonstrated the need for torpedo nets. The failure to have torpedo nets placed in front of the battleships was monumental. The U.S. Navy simply was not at all prepared for an air attack with torpedoes. They simply assumed that the shallow water (44 feet deep) of Pearl Harbor would not permit that type of an attack. In January, 1941, during a meeting, Admiral Kimmel suggested to Admiral Richardson that the Navy should consider utilizing torpedo nets in Pearl Harbor. When the Japanese torpedoes struck the battleships on December 7, 1941, it was a cruel irony that Kimmel was then in command of U.S. naval forces at Pearl Harbor. Admiral Kimmel became a victim of his own self-fulfilling prophecy. If there were torpedo nets in place, much of the disaster that occurred could have been avoided. As the battleships were aligned mostly two abreast in a row, it facilitated the Japanese attack. The battleships moored outward took the brunt of the attack and either were sunk or capsized due to numerous torpedo hits. The battleships moored inward received far less damage and none were sunk. Despite what Taranto showed the navies of the world, the U.S. Navy still clung to the belief that it was unnecessary to have torpedo nets, because the water was too shallow to accommodate a torpedo attack from the air. The American Navy was unaware that the Japanese had modified their torpedoes, by fitting them with wooden fins, thereby

45

making them extremely deadly even in the shallow waters of Pearl Harbor. If the torpedo nets were stationed in front of the ships, the torpedoes would have exploded prior to striking the battleships.

Ignoring the early warnings from the surface ships Antares and Ward that an attack was commencing and the observations of the radar installation that there was a large group of incoming aircraft approaching Oahu, were two additional fatal blunders. On December 7th, two warnings of the impending attack were received, one each by the Army and Navy, with both services either ignoring or disregarding the warnings.

At approximately 6:30 a.m., the Antares, a supply ship, was approaching Pearl Harbor. It spotted a submarine going into the forbidden defensive zone. The Antares' Captain notified the patrolling destroyer Ward. The Ward entered the defensive zone and observed a midget submarine. The Ward commenced fire with its four inch deck gun and sank the midget submarine (The wreck of this midget sub was found in 2002 and it confirmed the Ward's account). These were the first shots officially fired by the United States in World War II. The event was then reported to the Naval District's watch officer.

The second alarm occurred at approximately 7:02 a.m. (about one half hour after the Ward fired on the submarine). The two army radar operators, at the Opana station above Kahuka Point on Oahu's north shore, detected a large formation of planes on their radar screen, heading towards Oahu. After checking and rechecking the equipment they finally notified the watch officer at Fort Shafter. The watch officer erroneously assumed that the planes were a squadron of B-17's anticipated from California. He failed to

46

confirm this assumption. If he had determined the nature of the incoming aircraft, an alert could have been issued of an impending attack, in sufficient time to raise a defense.

The United States failed to maintain a program of long range reconnaissance aircraft scouting a pre-determined perimeter around Oahu. The United States Navy should have had reconnaissance aircraft flying in predetermined patterns, creating a defense perimeter around Oahu. If Oahu's naval base would have been assumed to be the center of a circle with a radius of 100 miles, then a search pattern employing twelve long range planes could have been utilized. Each plane would fly one hundred miles from Oahu, the center point, towards every thirty degree mark of the compass. After 100 miles, the planes would then turn right and proceed to the next thirty degrees mark, again turning right and returning to Pearl Harbor. As the exact flight time could be anticipated, when each plane made its first right turn, a new plane would take off from Pearl retracing the flight path of the original scout plane.

Had a search pattern such as this been employed, the U.S. military on Oahu would have been able to keep virtually the entire ocean and airspace around Oahu under visual observation for 100 miles in any direction. A defensive plan such as this would most likely have detected the incoming attacking aircraft and generated a warning in sufficient time for a viable defense to occur.

The Army commander, General Walter Short, believed the main danger to American aircraft would be sabotage, coming from Oahu's large native Japanese population. General Short became obsessed with the theory that the Japanese living on

47

Oahu were going to sabotage the land based aircraft. As a result of his obsession, he ordered that all planes were to be parked in close proximity to each other, to facilitate guarding them. Thusly, 230 bombers and fighters under his command were lined up in groups on the runways, to prevent attacks by saboteurs. Having all the planes bunched together, was the precipitous cause for most of the aircraft being destroyed in the attack. If the aircraft had been dispersed, it is plausible that a majority could have been unscathed by the attack. As it was, with all the planes bunched together, when one plane was hit and exploded, the explosion would cause all the adjacent planes to explode. The explosions emulated the pattern of falling dominos.

The failure to have defense aircraft either airborne or on alert and ready to take off at a moment's notice, negatively impacted on the ability to have a viable force ready to initiate an immediate defensive counter attack.

The United States War Department was complicit, by failing to keep its field commanders apprised of the deteriorating nature of the ongoing negotiations in Washington. They knew full well that an attack was imminent and they failed to notify Admiral Kimmel and General Short until it was far too late.

U.S. Army Intelligence had previously broken the Japanese diplomatic code and by Saturday night, December 6, 1941, they knew the Japanese were going to attack on or about December 7th, 1941. They failed to convey this information to the commanders in Oahu. By having no advance warning, General Short and Admiral Kimmel were unprepared for the attack contributing greatly to the horrendous loss of lives and ships.

THE MISTAKES MADE BY JAPAN

While the preceding failures of the United States exacerbated the damage caused by the Japanese attack, the Japanese committed more than their fair share of mistakes. The cumulative effect of these mistakes prevented the attack on Pearl Harbor from becoming the all-encompassing victory the Japanese had sought. Japan had hoped to strike such a devastating blow at Pearl Harbor, that the United States would be knocked out of the war before it started. Instead, due to Japanese failures, the United States though damaged and embarrassed by the attack, did not lose its ability to wage either an effective defensive or offensive war. In fact, its war machine was left so effectively unscathed by the Pearl Harbor attack, the United States was able to deal a death blow to Japan's aggressive naval war effort, a mere six months later at the Battle of Midway. Japanese failures at Pearl Harbor include:

- The failure of the Japanese to attack and destroy the American dry docks, piers and cranes, giving America the ability to quickly repair the damaged ships.

- The failure of the Japanese attack to destroy the American reserve oil supplies, this gave America the resources to fight a long range war

- The timidity of Admiral Nagumo inhibited aggressive actions during the attack, culminating with his failure to order a third strike

- Failing to conduct adequate reconnaissance and espionage prior to attacking, to verify that their primary targets, the American aircraft carriers, would be at Pearl Harbor when the attack occurred.

49

- Concentrating the attack on the old obsolete battleships, which were not threats to Japan's navy, while failing to recognize the importance of destroying the peripheral tools of war, including the oil tanks, oil reserves, and the oil tankers. If the tankers had been attacked and exploded, conceivably such an explosion could have destroyed the entire American fleet at anchor.

Tactically, the Japanese blundered nearly as badly as the Americans. Although the Americans thought their battleships to be the main striking arm of the fleet, it was the failure of the Japanese to destroy the carriers, submarines and oil tankers that left the U.S. with sufficient offensive capacity to counter attack.

The Japanese failed to inflict major damage to any of the permanent facilities, specifically the dry docks, storage tanks, piers, cranes, and airfields. The dry docks, piers, oil tanks and airfields were left relatively undamaged, leaving the U.S. with the tools to repair, regroup, and retaliate. The Japanese failed to bomb the United States dry docks, leaving the U.S. with the wherewithal to repair most of the ships damaged ships in the attack. Loss of the dry docks could have been a fatal blow to the United States war effort as the ability to timely repair the damaged ships would have been jeopardized or worse; eliminated.

Since all of the U.S. Navy's five commissioned tankers were in Pearl Harbor, had the Japanese attack destroyed them, the ability to perform long range actions would have been denied to the United States. One of the tankers, the Nehso, was full of gasoline. Had the Japanese followed through with a third wave attack and caused the Nehso to

50

explode, the force of such an explosion would have decimated most of the ships at anchor in the harbor.

Another very critical error made by Japan was the failure to strike the oil storage facilities. This could have been far more disastrous than the mere sinking of obsolete ships. Destruction of the oil tanks would have denied the U.S. the ability to maintain the remnants of its fleet at sea for sustained periods of time and simultaneously would have caused horrific damage by fire and explosion.

The attack leader, Mitsuo Fuchida, wanted to send a third wave of planes to finish the attack. Fleet Admiral Nagumo, disagreed with Fuchida and refused to order a third wave, thereby sealing Japan's fate to ultimately lose the war. If Fuchida's request would have been complied with, the destruction might have been complete and Japan would have been well on its way to victory in a short War. It is true that the Japanese would have lost a significant number of aircraft because the element of surprise was gone, but the loss and the risk were worth it, as the potential reward could have been absolute victory.

Admiral Nagumo did not have the killer instinct required to be a victor. He was more concerned with sustaining his fleet and preventing losses to his own fleet than he was with achieving complete victory. Had he been willing to take slightly greater risks he would have achieved far greater rewards. A little more aggressive action on Nagumo's part would have produced the absolute victory that dealt the death blow to the American Navy, which Admiral Yamamoto had sought. Admiral Nagumo's timidity left

51

Japan, fighting a superior opponent, temporarily on an equal basis. Nagumo's indecisiveness, lack of confidence, and timidity would continue to haunt Japan's war effort. These personality failures would ultimately lead to Japan's crushing defeat at the Battle of Midway, where it lost the capability to fight an offensive war.

After Pearl Harbor, Japan realized that it had merely equalized America's resources, temporarily, with theirs. They knew that as each day passed the American forces would gain in strength and resources, while theirs would diminish. The American war machine had the capability to deliver more men, material, and machinery to the conflict than the Japanese ever could. If Admiral Nagumo had ordered a third strike, the results of World War II may well have been different.

At the time of Pearl Harbor attack, the battleship had already become yesterday's weapon and the aircraft carrier was the offensive weapon of the present and future. By failing to determine that the American aircraft carriers would be in Pearl Harbor at the time of their attack, the Japanese failed to achieve the destruction of their real primary targets. In December 1941, the Americans enjoyed an overall superiority in carrier strength by having twelve carriers to Japan's nine. However, half of the American carriers were on duty in the Atlantic, thus, in actuality Japan held a superiority of nine to six carriers over America, in the Pacific. By failing to sink any carriers at Pearl Harbor, the Japanese merely maintained their slim numerically superiority in carriers and the Americans were left with a relatively intact capability to wage war. The Americans used this unimpaired offensive capability to meet and destroy a Japanese fleet containing four aircraft carriers, only six months later at the Battle of Midway, forever ending Japan's ability to make offensive war in the Pacific.

The Japanese were more concerned with attacking old outmoded battleships, which weren't a threat to their objectives, rather than attacking the more important strategic targets like the dry docks, oil tanks, tankers, cranes and air fields. Their failure to recognize the importance of attacking the oil reserves was a major blunder. The Japanese focused on destroying the military targets while ignoring strategic targets. If they would have focused on destroying both military and strategic targets the results obtained from the attack on Pearl Harbor could have been stupendous for Japan.

While Battleships remained in service, in varying roles, for another thirty plus years, their days as the lynchpins of the fleet were over. Henceforth, they would be reduced to subsidiary roles. They would become floating anti-aircraft defensive batteries for carriers, floating artillery for shore bombardments prior to invasions, and later mobile launching pads for missiles. The last head to head confrontation of battleships would occur in 1944 during the U.S. invasion of the Philippines. Subsequent to World War II, battleships, much like General MacArthur's "Old Soldiers", began to fade away and take their place in history.

BIKINI ATOLL

On September 2, 1945, World War II officially came to an end with the formal surrender of Japan, on the deck of the battleship USS Missouri BB63. The bittersweet irony of this event and its location was that it formally ended the battleship era, as well. While the Iowas would occasionally answer their country's call in the future and return to active duty until the 1990's, the battleship era was effectively over. The Iowa Class was designed to provide 50 years of service and that they did.

Subsequent to World War II, they were adapted to new roles and uses for the Navy. At first they became anti-aircraft platforms to protect carriers and also as floating artillery platforms for shore bombardment. However, even in these new capacities their usefulness and longevity were brief. As the combat airplane grew in sophistication and destructive power, the need for the Iowas was diminished. They were mothballed several times and recalled on multiple occasions, serving with distinction in Korea, Vietnam, and the Gulf War. When they were refitted in the 1980's, they fulfilled yet another purpose. The anti-aircraft guns were removed as were many of the 5 inch turrets and replaced with guided missile launching equipment. They sat comfortably offshore firing missiles and salvos from the sixteen inch guns at targets in Iraq.

By 1994, the four remaining Iowa Class battleships were all decommissioned and on their way to becoming war memorials and the battleship era was formally concluded.

19: USS MISSOURI BB63 FIRING A BROADSIDE AT TARGETS IN IRAQ DURING DESERT STORM

20: USS MISSOURI FIRING A TOMAHAWK MISSILE AT TARGETS IN IRAQ DURING DESERT STORM

At the conclusion of World War II, the United States Navy had amassed the largest fleet of ships the world had ever seen, numbering some 6,768 vessels. Included in the total were 28 aircraft carriers, 23 battleships, 71 escort carriers, 72 cruisers, 377 destroyers, 288 submarines, and several thousand support, supply, amphibious, and auxiliary vessels.

By 1943, the reality had set in that Japan would be defeated in the largest naval war ever fought. Many of the ships under construction, and most of the ships in service were destined be either obsolete or unnecessary, by the war's end. The concept of another naval war of this magnitude seemed at worst improbable and more likely was impossible. Thus, it was then understood, that a massive downsizing of the fleet would have to occur at the war's conclusion. This did take place in rapid order with the fleet of 6,768, vessels in August, 1945, going to:

- 1,248 in June, 1946,

- 842 in June, 1947,

- 737 in June, 1948,

- 690 in June, 1949, 634 by June, 1950.

A portion of this downsizing for battleships and other warships would take place during the nuclear bomb tests conducted at Bikini Atoll, under the code name Operations Crossroads, in July, 1946.

On July 1, 1946, some 95 vessels of the United States Navy were assembled at Bikini Atoll, a series of 30 plus islands comprising a mere dot on the surface of the Pacific

Ocean. Included in the flotilla were the old battleships, New York BB34, Arkansas BB33, Pennsylvania BB38, and Nevada BB36, the carriers Saratoga and Independence, 2 cruisers, 11 destroyers, 8 submarines and numerous other support ships. They were to be the targets for the testing of an atomic bomb, identical to the one dropped on Nagasaki. The bomb was dropped from a B-29 Super fortress named "Dave's Dream". This test was code named Able. The bomb named "Gilda", inflicted far less damage than was anticipated because it missed its target point by nearly one half mile. Only five ships were sunk, two transports, two destroyers, and one Japanese cruiser. The indomitable will and superior construction of the four American battleships allowed them to escape this test virtually unscathed.

Only July 25, 1946, the test known as Baker was conducted, utilizing an underwater bomb named "Helen of Bikini". Ten ships were either sunk or would eventually sink from damage sustained by the blast, including the old U.S. battleship Arkansas, the Japanese battleship Nagato, and the U.S. carrier Saratoga. The Arkansas BB33 was some 250 yards from the epi-center of the blast causing her hull to be crushed, she then capsized and sank. She now lies inverted, beneath the shallow waters of Bikini Atoll. The other three American battleships still remained afloat after this test. On July 31, 1948, the Nevada was used for gunnery target practice by the Iowa and other ships, still the Nevada failed to sink. She was finally sunk by an aerial launched torpedo. The Pennsylvania remained afloat until February 10, 1948 when she was sent to the bottom by naval gunfire. The New York having survived both nuclear tests was used as a target

57

vessel on July 6, 1948 and was sunk by a combination of naval gunfire and aerial bombs and torpedoes. Essentially, the Bikini Atoll tests showed that while the battleship, per se, was obsolete and no longer viable as a fighting ship, the American World War I vintage dreadnoughts were virtually indestructible.

The carnage of the blasts was so severe that they ended forever the concept, that large fleets of heavy surface ships could be an effective naval force, which started the next race to naval Armageddon, nuclear war at sea. The Cold War was intensifying and it would spawn a new and far more dreadful arms race, the naval nuclear arms race. The major combatants of the Cold War then set out to see who could build the biggest, most destructive, nuclear weapon and the best means of delivering it to the enemy.

What has followed is the age of the missile carrying nuclear propelled submarines. These vessels have so much destructive capability that they assumed the role of lynch-pin of our defensive strategy under the principle of "MAD", "mutually assured destruction". These nuclear missile carrying submarines are named after the various states of the union, having the honor once afforded to battleships.

The battleship era is over and it failed to teach the countries of the world the most important lesson of all, the only way to win an arms race is to not engage in one.

OVERVIEW OF THE UNITED STATES NAVY'S BATTLESHIPS

Of the 59 battleships commissioned by the United States Navy, only four were ever lost: the Utah BB31, the Arizona BB39, the Oklahoma BB37, and the Maine ACR1. The Maine was a victim of an explosion, initially, of undetermined origin. An official United States Naval Court of Inquiry had ruled that the ship was blown up by a mine, without directly placing the blame on Spain. It's sinking precipitated the Spanish American War. *"Remember the Maine"* became the rallying cry for the United States forces during the Spanish American War. The Maine was later raised by the United States Navy, towed out to sea and interred in a watery grave. In 1976, a team of American naval investigators concluded that the explosion of the Maine was likely caused by a fire started perhaps in a coal bunker that ignited its ammunition stores, not by a Spanish mine or act of sabotage as originally suspected.

The Utah BB31 was converted into an impotent gunnery target ship, in 1931, pursuant to the London Naval Treaty of 1930. Her armament was removed and many different types of anti-aircraft guns were added which were used for training. From 1931 to 1941 she served in a dual capacity, being used both as a target vessel and an anti-aircraft gunnery training vessel. Accordingly, she was declassified as BB31 and reclassified AG16.

The question then arises why did the Japanese attack and sink such a harmless vessel, when there were far more important targets in the harbor? The Utah was moored on the west side of Ford Island where the aircraft carriers Lexington and Saratoga would be moored, if in port.   It is believed that the Japanese were aware that both carriers were not in Pearl Harbor at the time of the attack.

21: USS UTAH BB31 SHOWN CAPSIZED AFTER THE ATTACK ON PEARL HARBOR

Apparently as a precautionary act, the Japanese sent a squadron of 16 Kate torpedo bombers towards Oahu from the Northwest, to approach Ford Island from the west.   If their intelligence was incorrect and the carriers were present they would have aircraft in place to attack them.   If their intelligence was correct and the carriers were not present, the attacking aircraft could then continue on into the harbor seeking other targets. For unknown reasons, the crews of two of the Kates fired their torpedoes at the Utah causing her to capsize and sink.   Most of the Utah's crew were able to successfully abandon ship, but 64 crewmen were killed, of which 58 were entombed in the Utah when she capsized.   In 1972, a memorial was erected in the vicinity of the wreck of the Utah.

The Arizona BB39 was peacefully at berth in Pearl Harbor when it was blown up by a single direct hit in its forward powder magazine. It was the victim of a 16.1 inch naval artillery shell that had been converted into a 1,757 pound aerial bomb. *"Remember the Arizona"* and "Remember Pearl Harbor" became two rallying cries for America during World War II. It is believed that the bomb was dropped by a Japanese Kate bomber, from the carrier Hiryu. America gained revenge when dive bombers from the USS Yorktown and USS Enterprise set the Hiryu on fire during the Battle of Midway, on June 4, 1942. The Hiryu was scuttled the next day as it was a decimated wreck, beyond any hope of being repaired or salvaged.

It took nine aerial torpedo hits to capsize and sink the Oklahoma BB37 during the Pearl Harbor attack. The Oklahoma, by virtue of its indomitable nature, was raised, refloated and made sea worthy during the salvage operations following the attack. It could be said that the act of refloating the Oklahoma was one of the ten greatest engineering feats of all time. There was not sufficient time to make her battle worthy, prior to the end of World War II, so she was sold for scrap. While under tow to the scrap yard, she became victim of a storm and sank 540 miles NE of Pearl Harbor. This was perhaps nature's way of giving an honorable warrior a more noble demise than the torches of the scrap yard.

All of the great naval powers lost one or more battleships to enemy gun fire during the great battles of World War I and World War II, but the United States was the only power never to suffer such a loss. The U.S. was the victor in perhaps the greatest naval war of all time, the Pacific Theater of World War II. There were many surface battles with the Japanese Navy but the results were all the same, heavy enemy losses, with the U.S. Battleships suffering no losses and only minor damage.

The United States Navy named its battleships after the states of the union. The only United States battleship not named for a state was USS Kearsarge BB5. The first ship named Kearsarge was a Mohican-class sloop-of-war, and is best known for her defeat of the Confederate commerce raider CSS Alabama during the American Civil War. Kearsarge was named for New Hampshire's Mount Kearsarge, with subsequent ships bearing this name being named after the 1861 Union sloop.

Every state had at least one commissioned battleship named for it except Montana. BB51 was to be named Montana after the state, but she was scrapped pursuant to the Washington Naval Treaty of 1923. Montana was also intended to be the name of the lead ship of a class of super Iowa's. They were intended to mount twelve 16 inch guns in four turrets of three and would have displaced nearly 80,000 tons when fully armed and manned. They were ordered in 1941 and plans were drawn. Their intended purpose was to be the class, heavy enough, to defeat the Japanese Navy's Yamato class. However, in 1943 the Navy reached the conclusion that the tide of battle had turned, the United States was going to defeat the Japanese and the Montanas were unnecessary as the battleship's days were ending. Thus, the orders were canceled on July 21, 1943.

In addition to Montana, neither Alaska nor Hawaii had a battleship named in their honor as both were territories during the Dreadnought Era. Instead, Alaska, Guam and

Hawaii were used as names for a class of battle cruisers CB1, CB2 and CB3, respectively. The Alaska and the Guam saw action in World War II while the Hawaii was still incomplete at the war's end. It was intended for there to be six vessels in this class. The others contemplated were the Philippines CB4, the Puerto Rico CB5 and the Samoa CB6. Orders for these three vessels were canceled in 1943, using the same thought process which sent the proposed Montana class to the scrap heap before they were ever built.

This was the only class of battle cruisers ever built for the United States Navy and the only class of battle cruisers built by any country after 1921. They were lighter, 32,500 tons, with smaller guns, nine 9 inch guns displayed in three turrets of three each, and less heavily armored than battleships. They were not, however, significantly bigger, faster, or better armed than heavy cruisers and hence did not meet the Navy's future plans and by 1960 all faced the cutter's torch.

The first battleships built for the United States Navy were the Texas ACR2 and Maine ACR1 but they were not true battleships. They were officially deemed second class battleships and never carried a "BB" designation for a hull number. They had non-centerline turrets. The Texas was decommissioned in 1911. The Texas class displaced approximately 6,500 tons, had twelve inch armor, and four 10 inch guns in two non-centerline turrets of two guns each.

The next group of pre-dreadnoughts was the three ships of the Indiana class, Indiana BB1, Massachusetts BB2, and Oregon BB3. These had low free boards making them unseaworthy for long journeys; hence they were dubbed "coastal battleships". They met their demise as gunnery targets on November 1, 1920.

The Indianas introduced centerline turrets to the United States Navy; they displaced approximately 10,000 tons, had eighteen inch armor and four 13 inch guns in two turrets of two each.

Next came the first Iowa class with the Iowa BB4, the Kearsarge class with Kearsarge BB5 and Kentucky BB6, and the Illinois class of Illinois BB7, Alabama BB8 and Wisconsin BB9, all displaced approximately 11,500 tons, had sixteen inch armor and four 13 inch guns, the Iowa BB4 was the only one with fourteen inch armor and 12 inch guns, in two turrets of two. This coal burning class introduced double deck superimposed turrets.

The next 16 battleships, BB10 to BB25 were essentially the same displacing between 15,000 and 16,000 tons, having 11 inch armor, with four 12 inch guns in two turrets of two. Mississippi BB23 and Idaho BB24 were the exceptions with 9 inch armor and a displacement of 13,000 tons, with both sold to Greece in July, 1914. The Idaho BB24 was the last pre-dreadnought commissioned on April 1, 1908. The eighteen pre-dreadnoughts BB5 to BB22 comprised Teddy Roosevelt's Great White Fleet which sailed around the world demonstrating to one and all that the United States Navy had come of age. Alabama BB8 and Maine BB10 were with the fleet from Hampton Roads, Virginia to San Francisco, California, but they dropped out of the fleet, in San Francisco, for repairs there. Then proceeded to conduct their own voyage around the world. Wisconsin BB9 and Nebraska BB14 joined the main fleet in San Francisco, and continued with the fleet on the main voyage. The main fleet always contained only 16 battleships. The South Carolina BB26 marked the United States entry into the Dreadnought Era and naval armament race. The first two dreadnought types, South Carolina BB26 and Michigan BB27, still only displaced 16,000 tons and had eleven inch armor, but their great innovation was having four turrets, each holding two 12 inch guns. The firepower of battleships had now doubled but the race was now on in earnest to see who could build the biggest one that could still float. Eventually the Japanese won this aspect of the race with the 80,000 ton Yamato Class that had nine 18 inch and six 6 inch guns.

The North Dakota class, North Dakota BB29, and the Utah class, Florida BB30 and Utah BB31 increased the size of battleships another notch from 20,000 to 24,000 tons. They still had eleven inch armor but armament increased to ten 12 inch guns that were maintained in five turrets of two each.

The Arkansas class – Arkansas BB33 and Wyoming BB32 displaced 26,000 tons, had eleven inch armor and six turrets of two 12 inch guns.

The second Texas class – New York BB34 and Texas BB35 improved to 27,000 tons, with twelve inch armor, and five turrets of two 14 inch guns each. This class was the last of the battleships to maintain all their big guns on one deck. The Texas is now a War Memorial at San Jacinto, Texas. The Texas is the only true Dreadnought surviving, being constructed prior to World War I. March 12, 2014 marked the one hundredth anniversary of its being commissioned. It is also the oldest "battleship now a war memorial".

The Nevada class – Nevada BB35 and Oklahoma BB36 ratcheted the race up yet another notch weighing in at 30,500 tons, having thirteen inch armor and twelve 14 inch guns in four turrets of three.

The final class of the World War I dreadnoughts was the Pennsylvania class of the Pennsylvania BB38 and Arizona BB39 which displaced 31,500 tons, with fourteen inch armor and twelve 14 inch guns in four turrets of three each. The wreck of the Arizona BB39 is now a war memorial in Pearl Harbor, dedicated to those who gave their lives so valiantly on that day which will live in infamy.

From the South Carolina BB26 to the Arizona BB39, battleships had basically doubled in displacement going from 16,000 to 31,500 tons, armor increased from eleven inches to fourteen inches, and armament went from eight 12 inch guns to twelve 14 inch guns. All this was accomplished in a mere six years, between March 1, 1910 and October 17, 1916.

Subsequent to World War I, the New Mexico class – New Mexico BB40, Mississippi BB41 and Idaho BB42 and the Tennessee class – Tennessee BB43 and California BB44 made their appearance. They were all essentially similar to the Pennsylvania class, displacing 32,000 tons, having fourteen inch armor and carrying twelve fourteen inch guns in four turrets of three.

Next was the Maryland class – Colorado BB45, Maryland BB46 and West Virginia BB48, which showed further innovation and improvement. Though they still displaced 32,000 tons, they boasted sixteen inch armor and eight 16 inch guns in four turrets of two each. The Washington BB47 was never completed (75.9% complete) and was broken up pursuant to the Washington Naval Conference of 1923.

At the time of the Washington Naval Treaty of 1923, the United States was in the process of building a class of light battleships or battle cruisers, intended to be the South Dakota BB49, Indiana BB50, Montana BB51, North Carolina BB52, Iowa BB53, and Massachusetts BB54. This was canceled and the ships never were finished.

As a result of the Washington Naval Treaty and successor treaties, there were no battleships commissioned, completed, or built by the United States from December 1, 1923, the West Virginia BB48, until April 9, 1941when the North Carolina BB55 went into service. The same was true for most of the navies of the world, though some countries notably Japan, Italy, and Germany launched battleships as early as 1939. Essentially, there were no new battleships constructed for nearly fifteen years.

It is likely that this hiatus from construction and innovation contributed to the battleships becoming effectively obsolete. A metamorphous was taking place, with the aircraft carrier replacing the battleship as the lynch-pin of the navies of the world. As countries tried to improve their defensive and offensive capabilities, they had to do so without being able to add battleships with improved technology to their fleets. Hence, they turned to new strategies and weaponry, with the most logical type of ship being the aircraft carrier and naval air warfare. The Washington Naval Treaty of 1923 simultaneously dealt a death blow to battleships and made aircraft carriers the queens of naval warfare, for the moment.

The North Carolinas BB55 and Washington BB56 displaced 44,800 tons had sixteen inch armor, and carried nine 16 inch guns.

They were followed by the South Dakotas – South Dakota BB57, Indiana BB58, Massachusetts BB59 and Alabama BB60 which were essentially similar in armament to the North Carolina Class, but shorter and squatter in appearance. They too displaced 44,500 tons, had sixteen inch armor, and nine 16 inch guns. The Massachusetts BB59 is now a War Memorial in Fall River, Massachusetts and the Alabama BB60 is a War Memorial in Mobile, Alabama.

The greatest accomplishment in battleship design and production was the Iowa class of the Iowa BB61, New Jersey BB62, Missouri BB63 and Wisconsin BB64. The Iowa class displaced 57,000 tons, had sixteen inch armor and carried nine 16 inch guns. The facet of their design which enabled them to become timeless and allowed them to serve their country for nearly fifty years was their speed. They were capable of sustaining 35 knots or better, thus, they were known as the "fast battleships". This allowed them to keep up with the attack carriers and provide much needed anti-aircraft fire to protect the new queens of the Navy. Their hulls and boilers were designed to last and provide useful service for fifty years or more and amazingly they did just that.

Six were ordered; BB61 Iowa, BB62 New Jersey, BB63 Missouri, BB64 Wisconsin, BB65 Illinois and BB66 Kentucky. These were the last of the battleships to ever be built. The Iowa BB61, New Jersey BB62, Missouri BB63 and Wisconsin BB64 all saw action in World War II. The Illinois BB65 and Kentucky BB66 were 20% and 73% complete, respectively, at the war's end and were never finished. The Kentucky BB66 was launched, incomplete in 1950 and was stricken on June 9, 1958. The order for the Illinois was canceled on August 11, 1945 and both vessels were broken up starting September, 1958. The remaining four Iowa's gave their country nearly fifty years of superior service. As these were the "fast" battleships designed to give escort to the carriers of WWII, they had the speed to hold their own with the modern fleets of today. One or more of the Iowa's served with distinction during the wars of two generations - World War II, Korea, Vietnam and the Gulf War. Under President Reagan the Iowa's were refitted for modern duty having missile batteries replace anti-aircraft guns and they returned to active duty between December 28, 1982 and May 10, 1986.

All have been decommissioned and have been turned into War Memorials. The Missouri BB63 is a War Memorial, berthed next to the sunken wreckage of the Arizona and her Memorial. Together they symbolize the beginning and end of World War II.

It was hoped that the other Iowa class ships, when the Navy would be finally through with them, would also become War Memorials. It would have been so wrong for these great ladies of the sea, who served their country so well, to suffer the ignominious disgrace of succumbing to the cutter's torch in a scrap yard. This hope was fulfilled when the Wisconsin BB64, New Jersey BB62 and Iowa BB61 became war memorials. These great machines of war now serve as museums like the Missouri BB63 in Pearl Harbor, with the Wisconsin BB64 in Norfolk, Virginia, the New Jersey BB62 in Camden, New Jersey and the last to be retired, the Iowa BB61, going to Los Angeles, California in 2012.

In addition to the four Iowas that are now war memorials, there are four other battleships retired as war memorials: Texas BB35 at San Jacinto, TX, North Carolina BB55 at Wilmington, NC, Massachusetts BB59, at Fall River MA, and Alabama BB60 at Mobile, Alabama.

These battleships now stand as living memorials to all the brave sailors who served on them and all the other sailors and ships in our naval history. Though they are no longer on active duty, they are the last of their kind and stirring reminders of what was the Dreadnought Era. All the rest of their kind perished long ago, vanishing forever from the surface of the world's oceans. Much like the last eight dinosaurs to roam the earth, they have now achieved complete and total mastery of their domain.

CHRONOLOGY OF THE UNITED STATES NAVY'S BATTLESHIPS

SECOND CLASS BATTLESHIPS

ACR1 - MAINE

22: USS MAINE ACR1 1898, COMMISSIONED SEPTEMBER 17, 1895, DECOMMISSIONED FEBRUARY 15, 1898.

EXPLODED IN HAVANA HARBOR FEBRUARY 15, 1898 PRECIPITATING THE SPANISH AMERICAN WAR

FOUR 10" GUNS IN TWO NON-CENTERLINE TURRETS

DISPLACING 6650 TONS

ARMOR 12 INCHES

CREW OF 362

SPEED 17 KNOTS

USS MAINE

23: WRECKAGE OF USS MAINE ACR1 AFTER IT EXPLODED IN CUBA

MAINE

24: RE-FLOATED WRECK OF USS MAINE ACR1 BEING TOWED TO SEA TO BE SUNK

ACR2 – TEXAS

25: USS TEXAS ACR2 CIRCA, COMMISSIONED AUGUST 15, 1895, DECOMMISSIONED FEBRUARY 11, 1911 AND SUNK AS A TARGET SHIP IN 1911.

FOUR 10" GUNS IN TWO NON-CENTERLINE TURRETS

DISPLACING 6650 TONS

ARMOR 12 INCHES

CREW OF 362

SPEED 17 KNOTS

PRE-DREADNOUGHT ERA

THE INDIANA CLASS - COASTAL BATTLESHIPS

BB1 – INDIANA

USS INDIANA (BB 1)

26: USS INDIANA BB1 COMMISSIONED NOVEMBER 20, 1895, DECOMMISSIONED JANUARY 31, 1919, SUNK AS A TARGET VESSEL NOVEMBER 1, 1920.   THE WRECK WAS SOLD FOR SCRAP ON MARCH 19, 1924

FOUR 13" GUNS IN TWO TWIN TURRETS

DISPLACING 10225 TONS

ARMOR 18 INCHES

CREW OF 473

SPEED 15 KNOTS

BB2 – MASSACHUSETTS

USS MASSACHUSETTS (BB 2)

27: USS MASSUSETTS BB2 COMMISIONED JUNE 10, 1896, WAS DECOMMISSIONED MAY 31, 1919, AND SUNK AS A TARGET VESSEL NOVEMBER 1, 1920. THE SHIP WAS NEVER SOLD FOR SCRAP. IN 1956 IT WAS CLAIMED BY THE STATE OF FLORIDA AND SINCE 1993 IT HAS BEEN THE FLORIDA UNDERWATER ARCHEOLOGICAL PRESERVE.

FOUR 13" GUNS IN TWO TWIN TURRETS

DISPLACING 10225 TONS

ARMOR 18 INCHES

CREW OF 473

SPEED 15 KNOTS

BB3 – OREGON

28: USS OREGON BB3 COMMISSIONED JULY 15, 1896, DECOMMISSIONED OCTOBER 4, 1919, AND WAS SOLD FOR SCRAP MARCH 15, 1956.

FOUR 13" GUNS IN TWO TWIN TURRETS

DISPLACING 10225 TONS

ARMOR 18 INCHES

CREW OF 473

SPEED 15 KNOTS

THE IOWA CLASS

BB4 – IOWA

29: USS IOWA BB4 COMMISSIONED JUNE 16, 1897, DECOMMISSIONED MARCH 31, 1919, AND SUNK AS A BOMBING TARGET IN 1923.   THE FIRST BATTLESHIP WITH DOUBLE DECK SUPERIMPOSED TURRETS.

FOUR 12" GUNS IN TWO TWIN TURRETS

DISPLACING 11410 TONS

ARMOR 14 INCHES

CREW OF 683

SPEED 17 KNOTS

THE KEARSARGE CLASS

BB5 – KEARSARGE

USS KEARSARGE (BB 5)

30: USS KEARSARGE BB5 COMMISSIONED FEBRUARY 20, 1900, DECOMMISSIONED MAY 18, 1920 AND WAS SCRAPPED AUGUST 9, 1955.   SHE WAS PART OF THE GREAT WHITE FLEET.

FOUR 13" GUNS IN TWO TWIN TURRETS

DISPLACING 11540 TONS

ARMOR 16 INCHES

CREW OF 554

SPEED 17 KNOTS

BB6 – KENTUCKY

31: USS KENTUCK BB6 COMMISSIONED MAY 15, 1900, DECOMMISSIONED MARCH 29, 1920, AND SOLD FOR SCRAP MARCH 23, 1923.   SHE WAS PART OF THE GREAT WHITE FLEET.

FOUR 13" GUNS IN TWO TWIN TURRETS

DISPLACING 11540 TONS

ARMOR 16 INCHES

CREW OF 554

SPEED 17 KNOTS

THE ILLINOIS CLASS

BB7 – ILLINOIS

32 : USS ILLINOIS BB7 COMMISSIONED SEPTEMBER 16, 1901, DECOMMISSIONED MAY 15, 1920 AND WAS

SOLD FOR SCRAP ON MAY 18, 1956.   SHE WAS PART OF THE GREAT WHITE FLEET.

FOUR 13" GUNS IN TWO TWIN TURRETS

DISPLACING 12250 TONS

ARMOR 16 INCHES

CREW OF 536

SPEED 16 KNOTS

BB8 – ALABAMA

33: USS ALABAMA BB8 COMMISSIONED OCTOBER 16, 1900, DECOMMISSIONED MAY 7, 1920 AND SUNK AS A TARGET VESSEL SEPTEMBER 27, 1921.   SHE WAS PART OF THE GREAT WHITE FLEET WHEN IT DEPARTED HAMPTON ROADS, VIRGINIA AND DROPPED OUT OF THE FLEET WHEN IT REACHED SAN FRANCISCO, CA FOR REPAIRS.

FOUR 13" GUNS IN TWO TWIN TURRETS

DISPLACING 12250 TONS

ARMOR 16 INCHES

CREW OF 536

SPEED 16 KNOTS

BB9 – WISCONSIN

34: USS WISCONSIN BB9 COMMISSIONED FEBRUARY 4, 1901, DECOMMISSIONED MAY 15, 1920, AND SCRAPPED IN JANUARY, 1922. JOINED THE GREAT WHITE FLEET IN SAN FRANCISCO, CA AS A REPLACEMENT FOR BB8 ALABAMA,

FOUR 13" GUNS IN TWO TWIN TURRETS

DISPLACING 12250TONS

ARMOR 16 INCHES

CREW OF 531

SPEED 16 KNOTS

THE MAINE CLASS

BB10 – MAINE

35: USS MAINE BB10 COMMISSIONED DECEMBER 29, 1902, DECOMMISSIONED MAY 15, 1920 AND SOLD FOR SCRAP JANUARY 26, 1922.   SHE WAS PART OF THE GREAT WHITE FLEET. DROPPED FROM THE FLEET WHEN IT REACHED SAN FRANCISCO, CA FOR REPAIRS

FOUR 12" GUNS IN TWO TWIN TURRETS

DISPLACING 12486 TONS

ARMOR 11 INCHES

CREW OF 561

SPEED 18 KNOTS

BB11 – MISSOURI

36: USS MISSOURI BB11 COMMISSIONED DECEMBER 1, 1903, DECOMMISSIONED SEPTEMBER 8, 1919 AND SCAPPED IN JANUARY, 1922.   SHE WAS PART OF THE GREAT WHITE FLEET.

FOUR 12" GUNS IN TWO TWIN TURRETS

DISPLACING 12362 TONS

ARMOR 11 INCHES

CREW OF 561

SPEED 18 KNOTS

BB12 – OHIO

37: USS OHIO BB12 COMMISSIONED OCTOBER 4, 1904, DECOMMISSIONED MAY, 31, 1922 AND SOLD FOR SCRAP MARCH, 1923.   SHE WAS PART OF THE GREAT WHITE FLEET.

FOUR 12" GUNS IN TWO TWIN TURRETS

DISPLACING 12723 TONS

ARMOR 11 INCHES

CREW OF 561

SPEED 18 KNOTS

THE VIRGINIA CLASS

BB13 – VIRGINIA

38: USS VIRGINIA BB13 COMMISSIONED MAY 7, 1906. DECOMMISSIONED AUGUST 13, 1920 AND SUNK AS A TARGET VESSEL ON SEPTEMBER 5, 1923.   SHE WAS PART OF THE GREAT WHITE FLEET.

FOUR 12" GUNS IN TWO TWIN TURRETS

DISPLACING 14948 TONS

ARMOR 11 INCHES

CREW OF 812

SPEED 19 KNOTS

BB14 – NEBRASKA

39: USS NEBRASKA BB14 COMMISSIONED JULY 1, 1907, DECOMMISSIONED JULY 2, 1920 AND SOLD FOR SCRAP ON NOVEMBER 9, 1923.   SHE WAS PART OF THE GREAT WHITE FLEET JOINING IT IN SAN FRANCISO CA AS A REPLACEMENT FOR BB10 MAINE.

FOUR 12" GUNS IN TWO TWIN TURRETS

DISPLACING 14948 TONS

ARMOR 11 INCHES

CREW OF 812

SPEED 19 KNOTS

BB15 – GEORGIA

40: USS GEORGIA BB15 COMMISSIONED SEPTEMBER 24, 1906, DECOMMISSIONED JULY 15, 1920 AND SOLD

FOR SCRAP NOVEMBER 10, 1923.   SHE WAS PART OF THE GREAT WHITE FLEET.

FOUR 12" GUNS IN TWO TWIN TURRETS

DISPLACING 14948 TONS

ARMOR 11 INCHES

CREW OF 812

SPEED 19 KNOTS

BB16 - NEW JERSEY

41: USS NEW JERSEY BB16 COMMISSIONED MAY 12, 1906, DECOMMISSIONED AUGUST 13, 1920 AND WAS SUNK AS A TARGET VESSEL ON SEPTEMBER 5, 1923.   SHE WAS PART OF THE GREAT WHITE FLEET.

FOUR 12" GUNS IN TWO TWIN TURRETS

DISPLACING 14948 TONS

ARMOR 11 INCHES

CREW OF 812

SPEED 19 KNOTS

BB17 - RHODE ISLAND

42: USS RHODE ISLAND BB17 COMMISSIONED FEBRUARY 19, 1906, DECOMMISSIONED JUNE 30, 1920 AND SOLD FOR SCRAP NOVEMBER 1, 1923.   SHE WAS PART OF THE GREAT WHITE FLEET.

FOUR 12" GUNS IN TWO TWIN TURRETS

DISPLACING 14948 TONS

ARMOR 11 INCHES

CREW OF 812

SPEED 19 KNOTS

THE CONNECTICUT CLASS

BB18 – CONNECTICUT

43 : USS CONNECTICUT BB18 COMMISSIONED SEPTEMBER 29, 1906, DECOMMISSIONED MARCH 1, 1923 AND SOLD FOR SCRAP NOVEMBER 1, 1923.   SHE WAS PART OF THE GREAT WHITE FLEET.

FOUR 12" GUNS IN TWO TWIN TURRETS

DISPLACING 16000 TONS

ARMOR 11 INCHES

CREW OF 827

SPEED 18 KNOTS

BB19 – LOUISIANA

44: USS LOUSIANNA BB19 COMMISSIONED JUNE 2, 1906, DECOMMISSIONED OCTOBER 20, 1920 AND WAS SOLD FOR SCRAP NOVEMBER 1, 1923.   SHE WAS PART OF THE GREAT WHITE FLEET.

FOUR 12" GUNS IN TWO TWIN TURRETS

DISPLACING 16000 TONS

ARMOR 11 INCHES

CREW OF 827

SPEED 18 KNOTS

BB20 - VERMONT

45: USS VERMONT BB20 COMMISSIONED MARCH 4, 1907, DECOMMISSIONED JUNE 30, 1920 AND WAS SOLD

FOR SCRAP NOVEMBER 10, 1923.   SHE WAS PART OF THE GREAT WHITE FLEET.

FOUR 12" GUNS IN TWO TWIN TURRETS

DISPLACING 16000 TONS

ARMOR 11 INCHES

CREW OF 827

SPEED 18 KNOTS

BB21 – KANSAS

46: USS KANSAS BB21 COMMISSIONED APRIL 18, 1907, DECOMMISSIONED DECEMBER 16, 1921 AND WAS SOLD FOR SCRAP AUGUST 24,, 1923.   SHE WAS PART OF THE GREAT WHITE FLEET.

FOUR 12" GUNS IN TWO TWIN TURRETS

DISPLACING 16000 TONS

ARMOR 11 INCHES

CREW OF 827

SPEED 18 KNOTS

BB22 – MINNESOTA

47: USS MINNESOTA BB22 COMMISSIONED MARCH 9, DECOMMISSIONED DECEMBER 1, 1921 AND WAS SOLD FOR SCRAP JANUARY 23, 1924.   SHE WAS PART OF THE GREAT WHITE FLEET.

FOUR 12" GUNS IN TWO TWIN TURRETS

DISPLACING 16000 TONS

ARMOR 11 INCHES

CREW OF 827

SPEED 18 KNOTS

BB25 - NEW HAMPSHIRE

48: USS NEW HAMPSHIRE BB25 COMMISSIONED MARCH 19, 1908, DECOMMISSIONED ON MAY 21, 1921 AND WAS SOLD FOR SCRAP NOVEMBER 10, 1923.

FOUR 12" GUNS IN TWO TWIN TURRETS

DISPLACING 16000 TONS

ARMOR 11 INCHES

CREW OF 827

SPEED 18 KNOTS

THE MISSISSIPPI CLASS

BB23 – MISSISSIPPI

49: USS MISSISSIPPI BB23 COMMISSIONED FEBRUARY 1, 1908, DECOMMISSIONED JULY 21, 1914 AND SOLD

TO GREECE IN JULY 21, 1914 AND RENAMED THE KILKIS

FOUR 12" GUNS IN TWO TWIN TURRETS

DISPLACING 13000 TONS

ARMOR 9 INCHES

CREW OF 744

SPEED 17 KNOTS

50: USS MISSISSIPPI BB23 AS SHOWN KILKIS, SUNK BY GERMAN DIVE BOMBERS APRIL 10, 1941. HER SISTER SHIP THE USS IDAHO BB24 RENAMED LEMNOS SUNK IN BACKGROUND.

51: USS IDAHO BB24 WAS SOLD TO GREECE IN 1914, RENAMED THE LEMNOS SHOWN FLYING GREEK FLAG.

BB24 – IDAHO

52: USS IDAHO BB24 COMMISSIONED APRIL 1, 1908, DECOMMISSIONED JULY 30, 1914 AND WAS SOLD TO GREECE JULY 30, 1914.

FOUR 12" GUNS IN TWO TWIN TURRETS

DISPLACING 13000 TONS

ARMOR 9 INCHES

CREW OF 744

SPEED 17 KNOTS

THE DREADNOUGHT ERA

THE SOUTH CAROLINA CLASS

BB26 - SOUTH CAROLINA

53: USS SOUTH CAROLINA BB26 COMMISSIONED MARCH 1, 1910, DECOMMISSIONED DECEMBER 15, 1921, SOLD FOR SCRAP APRIL 24, 1924. FIRST CLASS OF U.S. DREADNOUGHTS NAMED AFTER HER.

EIGHT 12" GUNS IN FOUR TWIN TURRETS

DISPLACING 16000 TONS

ARMOR 12INCHES

CREW OF 869

SPEED 19 KNOTS

BB27 – MICHIGAN

54: USS MICHIGAN BB27 COMMISSIONED JANUARY 4, 1910, DECOMMISSIONED FEBRUARY 22, 1922, SOLD FOR SCRAP NOVEMBER 10, 1923.   SHE WAS THE FIRST U.S. DREADNOUGHT COMMISSIONED.

EIGHT 12" GUNS IN FOUR TWIN TURRETS

DISPLACING 16000 TONS

ARMOR 11 INCHES

CREW OF 818

SPEED 19 KNOTS

BB28 – DELAWARE

55: USS DELAWARE BB28 COMMISSIONED APRIL 4, 1910, DECOMMISSIONED NOVEMBER 10, 1923, SOLD FOR SCRAP FEBRUARY 5, 1924.

TEN 12" GUNS IN FIVE TWIN TURRETS

DISPLACING 22000 TONS

ARMOR 11 INCHES

CREW OF 933

SPEED 21 KNOTS

BB29 - NORTH DAKOTA

56: USS NORTH DAKOTA BB29 COMMISSIONED APRIL 11, 1910, DECOMMISSIONED NOVEMBER 22, 1923, CONVERTED TO TARGET SHIP 1924, SOLD FOR SCRAP JANUARY 7, 1931.

TEN 12" GUNS IN FIVE TWIN TURRETS

DISPLACING 22000 TONS

ARMOR 11 INCHES

CREW OF 933

SPEED 21 KNOTS

THE UTAH CLASS

BB30 – FLORIDA

57: USS FLORIDA BB30 COMMISSIONED SEPTEMBER 15, 1911, DECOMMISIONED FEBRUARY 16, 1931, SCRAPPED 1932.

TEN 12" GUNS IN FIVE TWIN TURRETS

DISPLACING 23000 TONS

ARMOR 11 INCHES

CREW OF 1001

SPEED 21 KNOTS

BB31 – UTAH

58: USS UTAH BB31 COMMISSIONED AUGUST 31, 1911, DECOMMISSIONED NOVEMBER 13, 1944, CONVERTED TO TARGET VESSEL 1931, SUNK AT PEARL HARBOR DECEMBER 7, 1941.

TEN 12" GUNS IN FIVE TWIN TURRETS

DISPLACING 21825 TONS

ARMOR 11 INCHES

CREW OF 1001

SPEED 21 KNOTS

THE ARKANSAS CLASS

BB32 – WYOMING

59: USS WYOMING BB32 COMMISSIONED SEPTEMBER 25, 1912, DECOMMISSIONED AUGUST 1, 1947, CONVERTED TO TRAINING SHIP 1931, SCRAPPED OCTOBER 30, 1947.

TWELVE 12" GUNS IN SIX TWIN TURRETS

DISPLACING 26000 TONS

ARMOR 11 INCHES

CREW OF 1063

SPEED 21 KNOTS

BB33 – ARKANSAS

60: USS ARKANSAS BB33 COMMISSIONED SEPTEMBER 17, 1912, DECOMMISSIONED JULY 25, 1946, WAS A TARGET IN BOTH THE BIKINI ATOLL NUCLEAR TESTS OF JULY, 1946.   SHE WAS SUNK BY THE UNDERWATER BLAST OF TEST BAKER ON JULY 25, 1946.

TWELVE 12" GUNS IN SIX TWIN TURRETS

DISPLACING 26000 TONS

ARMOR 11 INCHES

CREW OF 1063

SPEED 21 KNOTS

THE NEW YORK CLASS

BB34 - NEW YORK

61: USS NEW YORK BB34 COMMISSIONED MAY 15, 1914, DECOMMISSIONED AUGUST 29, 1946, DECOMMISSIONED JULY 25, 1946, A TARGET IN BOTH THE BIKINI ATOLL NUCLEAR TESTS OF JULY, 1946, EVENTUALLY SUNK AS A TARGET SHIP ON JULY 6, 1948

TEN 14" GUNS IN FIVE TWIN TURRETS

DISPLACING 27000 TONS

ARMOR 12 INCHES

CREW OF 1042

SPEED 21 KNOTS

BB35 – TEXAS

62: USS TEXAS BB35 COMMISSIONED MARCH 12, 1914, DECOMMISSIONED AUGUST 21, 1948, BECAME A WAR MEMORIAL ON APRIL 21, 1948, NOW LOCATED AT SAN JACINTO, TEXAS.

TEN 14" GUNS IN FIVE TWIN TURRETS

DISPLACING 27000 TONS

ARMOR 12 INCHES

CREW OF 1042

SPEED 21 KNOTS

THE NEVADA CLASS

BB36 – NEVADA

63: USS NEVADA BB36 COMMISSIONED MARCH 11, 1916, AUGUST 29, 1946, SURVIVED BOTH OF THE NUCLEAR TESTS AT BIKINI ATOLL IN JULY, 1946.   FINALLY SUNK BY NAVAL GUNFIRE JULY 31, 1948.

TEN 14" GUNS IN TWO TWIN TURRETS SUPERIMPOSED ON TWO TURRETS OF THREE

DISPLACING 30500 TONS

ARMOR 13 INCHES

CREW OF 2220, IN 1945

SPEED 20 KNOTS

BB37 – OKLAHOMA

64: USS OKLAHOMA BB37 COMMISSIONED MAY 2, 1916, DECOMMISSIONED SEPTEMBER 1, 1944 CAPSIZED

DURING ATTACK ON PEARL HARBOR, REFLOATED, SOLD FOR SCRAP 1947, SUNK DURING A STORM WHILE

BE TOWED TO SCRAP YARD MAY 17, 1947.

TEN 14" GUNS IN TWO TWIN TURRETS SUPERIMPOSED ON TWO TURRETS OF THREE

DISPLACING 29000 TONS

ARMOR 13 INCHES

CREW OF 1398, IN 1929

SPEED 20 KNOTS

THE PENNSYLVANIA CLASS

BB38 – PENNSYLVANIA

65: USS PENNSYLVANIA BB38 COMMISSIONED JUNE 12, 1916, SHE WAS A TARGET OF BOTH OF THE NUCLEAR TESTS AT BIKINI ATOLL IN JULY, 1946 AND WAS DECOMMISSIONED AUGUST 29, 1946. SHE WAS FINALLY SUNK BY NAVAL GUNFIRE ON FEBRUARY 10, 1948, OFF OF KWAJALEIN ATOLL.

TWELVE 14" GUNS IN TWO TURRETS OF THREE SUPERIMPOSED ON TWO TURRETS OF THREE

DISPLACING 31400 TONS

ARMOR 14 INCHES

CREW OF 1358

SPEED 21 KNOTS

BB39 – ARIZONA

66: USS ARIZONA BB39 COMMISSIONED OCTOBER 17, 1916, STILL ON ACTIVE DUTY ROSTER, SUNK PEARL

HARBOR DECEMBER 7, 1941, WRECKAGE PRESERVED AS WAR MEMORIAL.

TWELVE 14" GUNS IN TWO TURRETS OF THREE SUPERIMPOSED ON TWO TURRETS OF THREE

DISPLACING 31900 TONS

ARMOR 14 INCHES

CREW OF 1512

SPEED 21 KNOTS

67: USS ARIZONA BB39 WRECKAGE BURNING AFTER EXPLODING FROM AERIAL BOMB HIT DURING ATTACK

ON PEARL HARBOR

THE NEW MEXICO CLASS

BB40 - NEW MEXICO

68: USS NEW MEXICO BB40 COMMISSIONED MAY 20, 1918, DECOMMISSIONED JULY 19, 1946, SCRAPPED NOVEMBER 9, 1947.

TWELVE 14" GUNS IN TWO TURRETS OF THREE SUPERIMPOSED ON TWO TURRETS OF THREE

DISPLACING 32000 TONS

ARMOR 14 INCHES

CREW OF 1930

SPEED 23 KNOTS

BB41 - MISSISSIPPI

69: USS MISSISSIPPI BB41 COMMISSIONED DECEMBER 18, 1917, DECOMMISSIONED SEPTEMBER 17, 1956, CONVERTED TO TRIALS SHIP 1946, SCRAPPED NOVEMBER 28, 1956.

TWELVE 14" GUNS IN TWO TURRETS OF THREE SUPERIMPOSED ON TWO TURRETS OF THREE

DISPLACING 32000 TONS

ARMOR 14 INCHES

CREW OF 1930

SPEED 23 KNOTS

BB42 – IDAHO

70: USS IDAHO BB42 COMMISSIONED MARCH 24, 1919, DECOMMISSIONED FEBRRUARY 14, 1947, SOLD FOR SCRAP NOVEMBER 24, 1947.

TWELVE 14" GUNS IN TWO TURRETS OF THREE SUPERIMPOSED ON TWO TURRETS OF THREE

DISPLACING 32000 TONS

ARMOR 14 INCHES

CREW OF 1930

SPEED 23 KNOTS

THE TENNESSEE CLASS

BB43 – TENNESSEE

71: USS TENNESSEE BB43 COMMISSIONED JUNE 3, 1920, DECOMMISSIONED FEBRUARY 14, 1947, MOTHBALLED, SCRAPPED JULY 10, 1959, SHOWN AS REFITTED CIRCA 1943.

TWELVE 14" GUNS IN TWO TURRETS OF THREE SUPERIMPOSED ON TWO TURRETS OF THREE

DISPLACING 33000 TONS

ARMOR 14 INCHES

CREW OF 2129

SPEED 21 KNOTS

BB44 – CALIFORNIA

72: USS CALIFORNIA BB44 COMMISSIONED AUGUST 10, 1921, DECOMMISSIONED FEBRUARY 14, 1947, MOTHBALLED, SCRAPPED JULY 10, 1959.

TWELVE 14" GUNS IN TWO TURRETS OF THREE SUPERIMPOSED ON TWO TURRETS OF THREE

DISPLACING 32600 TONS, 40950 AFTER BEING REFITTED

ARMOR 14 INCHES

CREW OF 2129

SPEED 21 KNOTS

THE COLORADO CLASS

BB45 – COLORADO

73: USS COLORADO BB45 COMMISSIONED AUGUST 30, 1923, DECOMMISSIONED JANUARY 7, 1947, THEN

MOTHBALLED, AND FINALLY SCRAPPED ON JULY 23,1959.

EIGHT 16" GUNS IN TWO TWIN TURRETS OF TWO, SUPERIMPOSED ON TWIN TURRETS TWO

DISPLACING 32500 TONS

ARMOR 14 INCHES

CREW OF 2100

SPEED 21 KNOTS

74: USS MARYLAND BB46 COMMISSIONED JULY 21, 1921, DECOMMISSIONED APRIL 3, 1947, SOLD FOR SCRAP JULY 8, 1959.

EIGHT 16" GUNS IN TWO TWIN TURRETS OF TWO, SUPERIMPOSED ON TWIN TURRETS TWO

DISPLACING 32500 TONS

ARMOR 13.5 INCHES

CREW OF 2100

SPEED 21 KNOTS

75: USS WASHINGTON BB47 STRUCK FEBRUARY 8, 1922, INCOMPLETE WORK HALTED FEBRUARY 8, 1922

PER THE NAVAL TREATY OF 1923, SUNK BY GUN FIRE NOVEMBER 25, 1924.

BB48 - WEST VIRGINIA

76: USS WEST VIRGINIA BB48 COMMISSIONED DECEMBER 1, 1923, DECOMMISSIONED JANUARY 9, 1947, MOTHBALLED, SCRAPPED AUGUST 4, 1959.

EIGHT 16" GUNS IN TWO TWIN TURRETS OF TWO, SUPERIMPOSED ON TWIN TURRETS TWO

DISPLACING 32100 TONS

ARMOR 13.5 INCHES

CREW OF 2100

SPEED 21 KNOTS

SCRAPPED PURSUANT TO THE WASHINGTON TREATY OF 1923

THE SOUTH DAKOTA CLASS

BB49 - SOUTH DAKOTA

USS South Dakota BB49 was commissioned March 15, 1920, construction was canceled at 38.5% complete, and she was sold for scrap on October 25, 1923, with the scrapping completed on November 15, 1924

BB50 – INDIANA

USS Indiana BB50 commissioned November 1, 1920, canceled at 34 % complete, was struck October 25, 1923 and was scrapped on the slip.

BB51 – MONTANA

USS Montana BB51 commissioned September 1, 1920, canceled at 27.6% complete, was struck August 24, 1923, and was sold for scrap October 25, 1923.

BB52 - NORTH CAROLINA

USS North Carolina BB52 commissioned January 12, 1920, canceled at 36.7% complete, struck November 10, 1923, and was sold for scrap October 25, 1923.

BB53 – IOWA

USS Iowa BB53 commissioned May 17, 1920, canceled at 31.8% complete, struck November 10, 1923, and was sold for scrap November 8, 1923.

BB54 – MASSACHUSETTS

USS Massachusetts BB54 commissioned April 4, 1921, canceled at 11% complete, struck November 10, 1923, and was sold for scrap November 8, 1923.

THE FAST BATTLESHIPS OF WORLD WAR II

THE NORTH CAROLINA CLASS

BB55 - NORTH CAROLINA

77: USS NORTH CAROLINA BB55 COMMISSIONED APRIL 9, 1941, DECOMMISSIONED JUNE 27, 1947, STRICKEN JUNE 1, 1960, SAVED AS WAR MEMORIAL LOCATED IN WILMINGTON, NORTH CAROLINA.

NINE 16" GUNS IN THREE TURRETS OF THREE

DISPLACING 44800 TONS

ARMOR 16 INCHES

CREW OF 2339

SPEED 27 KNOTS

BB56 – WASHINGTON

78: USS WASHINGTON BB56 COMMISSIONED MAY 15, 1941, DECOMMISSIONED JUNE 27, 1947, STRICKEN JUNE 1, 1960, SCRAPPED MAY 24, 1961.

NINE 16" GUNS IN THREE TURRETS OF THREE

DISPLACING 44800 TONS

ARMOR 16 INCHES

CREW OF 1989

SPEED 27 KNOTS

THE SOUTH DAKOTA CLASS

BB57 - SOUTH DAKOTA

79: USS SOUTH DAKOTA BB57 COMMISSIONED MARCH 20, 1942, DECOMMISSIONED JANUARY 31, 1947, SCRAPPED OCTOBER 25, 1962.

NINE 16" GUNS IN THREE TURRETS OF THREE

DISPLACING 44500 TONS

ARMOR 16 INCHES

CREW OF 1793

SPEED 27 KNOTS

BB58 - INDIANA

80: USS INDIANA BB58 COMMISSIONED APRIL 30, 1942, DECOMMISSIONED SEPTEMBER 11, 1947, SCRAPPED OCTOBER 23, 1963.

NINE 16" GUNS IN THREE TURRETS OF THREE

DISPLACING 44500 TONS

ARMOR 16 INCHES

CREW OF 1793

SPEED 27 KNOTS

BB59 – MASSACHUSETTS

81: USS MASSACHUSETS BB59 COMMISSIONED MAY 12, 1942, DECOMMISSIONED MARCH 27, 1947, STRICKEN JUNE 1, 1962. SHE BECAME A WAR MEMORIAL AUGUST 14, 1965, NOW LOCATED IN FALLRIVER, MASSACHUSSETS.

NINE 16" GUNS IN THREE TURRETS OF THREE

DISPLACING 44500 TONS

ARMOR 16 INCHES

CREW OF 1793

SPEED 27 KNOTS

BB60 – ALABAMA

82: USS ALABAMA BB60 COMMISSIONED AUGUST 16, 1942, DECOMMISSIONED JANUARY 9, 1947, STRICKEN

JUNE 1, 1962.   SHE BECAME A WAR MEMORIAL JULY 7, 1964.   SHE IS NOW LOCATED IN MOBILE, ALABAMA.

NINE 16" GUNS IN THREE TURRETS OF THREE

DISPLACING 44500 TONS

ARMOR 16 INCHES

CREW OF 1793

SPEED 27 KNOTS

THE IOWA CLASS

BB61 – IOWA

83: USS IOWA BB61 COMMISSIONED FEBRUARY 22, 1943, DECOMMISSIONED OCTOBER 26, 1990, STRICKEN MARCH 17, 2006.   SHE IS NOW A WAR MEMORIAL LOCATED LOS ANGELES, CALIFORNIA.

NINE 16" GUNS IN THREE TURRETS OF THREE

DISPLACING 57000 TONS

ARMOR 16 INCHES

CREW OF 2700 DURING KOREAN WAR, CREW OF 1800 AFTER REFIT IN 1980's

SPEED 35 KNOTS

BB62 - NEW JERSEY

84: USS NEW JERSEY BB62 COMMISSIONED MAY 23, 1943, DECOMMISSIONED FEBRUARY 8, 1991, STRICKEN JANUARY 4, 1999. SHE IS NOW A WAR MEMORIAL LOCATED CAMDEN, NEW JERSEY.

NINE 16" GUNS IN THREE TURRETS OF THREE

DISPLACING 57000 TONS

ARMOR 16 INCHES

CREW OF 2700 DURING KOREAN WAR, CREW OF 1921 AFTER REFIT IN 1980's

SPEED 35 KNOTS

133

BB63 – MISSOURI

85: USS MISSOURI BB63 COMMISSIONED JUNE 11, 1944, DECOMMISSIONED MARCH 31, 1992, STRICKEN JANUARY 12, 1995.   SHE IS NOW A WAR MEMORIAL LOCATED HONOLULU, HAWAII.

NINE 16" GUNS IN THREE TURRETS OF THREE

DISPLACING 57000 TONS

ARMOR 16 INCHES

CREW OF 2700 DURING WORLD WAR II, CREW OF 1851 AFTER REFIT IN 1980's

SPEED 35 KNOTS

BB64 – WISCONSIN

86: USS WISCONSIN BB64 COMMISSIONED APRIL 16, 1944, DECOMMISSIONED SEPTEMBER 30, 1991, STRICKEN MARCH 17, 2006.   SHE IS NOW A WAR MEMORIAL LOCATED NORFOLK, VIRGINIA.

NINE 16" GUNS IN THREE TURRETS OF THREE

DISPLACING 57000 TONS

ARMOR 16 INCHES

CREW OF 2534 DURING WORLD WAR II, CREW OF 1566 AFTER REFIT IN 1980's

SPEED 35 KNOTS

87: USS ILLINOIS BB65 COMMISSIONED AUGUST 11, 1945 - CANCELED 22% COMPLETE, STRICKEN AUGUST 12, 1945.

BB66 – KENTUCKY

88: USS KENTUCKY BB66 COMMISSIONED JANUARY 12, 1950, CANCELED 73% COMPLETE, STRICKEN JUNE

9, 1958, SOLD FOR SCRAP OCTOBER 31, 1958.

THE INTENDED THAT NEVER WERE

THE MONTANA CLASS

BB67 – MONTANA

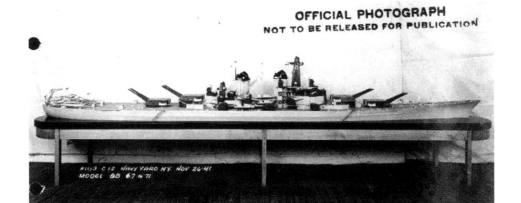

89: USS MONTANA BB67 COMMISSIONED JANUARY 1, 1941, CANCELED JULY 21, 1943, NEVER BUILT.

MONTANA CLASS AS PLANNED:

TWELVE 16" GUNS IN FOUR TURRETS OF THREE

DISPLACING 71000 TONS

ARMOR 16 TO 22 INCHES

CREW OF 2355 STANDARD, 2789 FLAGSHIP

SPEED 28 KNOTS

BB68 OHIO, BB69 MAINE, BB70 NEW HAMPSHIRE, BB71 LOUISIANA

All six were commissioned January 1, 1941, canceled July 21, 1943 and never built.

THE BATTLE CRUISERS

THE ALASKA CLASS

CB1 – ALASKA

90: USS ALASKA CB1 COMMISSIONED JUNE 17, 1944, DECOMMISSIONED FEBRUARY 17, 1947, STRICKEN JUNE 1, 1960, SOLD FOR SCRAP JUNE 30, 1961.

NINE 12" GUNS IN THREE TURRETS OF THREE

DISPLACING 32500 TONS

ARMOR 9 INCHES

CREW OF 1979

SPEED 33 KNOTS

CB2 – GUAM

91: USS GUAM CB2 COMMISSIONED JUNE 17, 1944, DECOMMISSIONED FEBRUARY 17, 1947, STRICKEN JUNE 1, 1960, SOLD FOR SCRAP MAY 24, 1961.

NINE 16" GUNS IN THREE TURRETS OF THREE

DISPLACING 32500 TONS

ARMOR 16 INCHES

CREW OF 1979

SPEED 35 KNOTS

CB3 – HAWAII

92: USS HAWAII CB3 COMMISSIONED SEPTEMBER 1, 1940 - NEVER FINISHED, STRICKEN JUNE 9, 1958, SOLD FOR SCRAP APRIL 15, 1959.

CB4 – PHILIPPINES, CB5 - PUERTO RICO, CB6 – SAMOA

ALL THREE WERE COMMISSIONED SEPTEMBER 1, 1940, CANCELED JUNE 24, 1943.

BIBLIOGRAPHY

Batchelor, John and Chant, Chris.   The Complete Encyclopedia of Warships.   Lisse, the Netherlands; Rebo International, 2007.

McCurtie, Francis E.   Jane's Fighting Ships of World War II.   Mishawaka, Indiana, Random House 1989.

Moore, Captain John E., RN.   Jane's Fighting Ships of World War I.   New York, New York, Military Press, 1990.

Newhart, Max R.   American Battleships.   Missoula, Montana; Pictorial Histories Publishing, 1995.

Whitly, M. J.   Battleships of World War Two – An International Encyclopedia.   Annapolis, Maryland; Naval Institute Press, 1998.

All other data and all photographs were gleaned from the public domain.

AUTHOR'S BIOGRAPHY

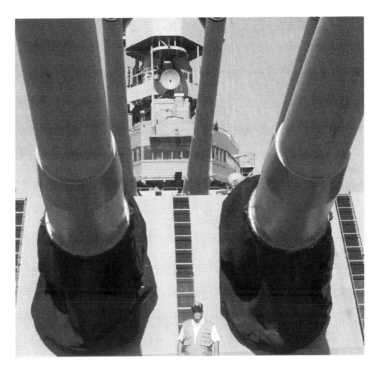

93 AUTHOR STANDING IN FRONT OF THE FORWARD TURRET OF THE USS WISCONSIN BB64, A WAR MEMORIAL IN NORFOLK, VA

Arthur C. "Art" Unger was born in Brooklyn, NY and currently resides in Wilmington, NC with his wife Grace and their two dogs George a reddish brown Dachshund and Libbie a black Chihuahua.

He graduated from Brooklyn College, with a BS in Accounting. He worked for American Airlines, Butler Aviation International, and ABC Air Freight, ran a private accounting practice, a financial consulting company, and owned a commercial collection agency. He is currently retired.

As a teenager Art became obsessed with battleships and the battleship era after viewing the movie "Sink the Bismarck", in 1960. The size, might, and awesome destructive power of battleships was indelibly etched into his thoughts from that moment on. Later in life he began a quest to obtain photographs and statistics on all the battleships ever to serve in the United States Navy. This was an arduous task for many years having more blank spots than completions, however, with the advent of the internet the task became far easier and was finally completed, culminating in this tome.

In addition to the study of battleships, Art enjoys making and finishing 1:1200 scale models of battleships, in this scale one inch equals one hundred feet. The models are made of pewter or lead, they have many moveable parts including main turrets, catapults, masts, and hoists, and to finish them he hand paints the ships to replicate how they actually appeared.

Additionally, he has a fascination/obsession with George Armstrong Custer and the Battle of the Little Big Horn that began with a book report he prepared in the fourth grade.   He has since spent over fifty years trying to unravel the mystery which shrouds the events that occurred on June 25, 1876.

The author was one of the foremost private collectors of Custerianna. His collection included a vast library, with many rare first editions, artifacts, autographs, and letters. Unfortunately the collection was destroyed in a catastrophic house fire.

In addition to Battleships and George Custer and the Battle of the Little Bighorn, his areas of study include the United States Civil War, United States Naval History, Medieval and Tudor English History.

Arthur C. Unger has previously written and published three books regarding George Armstrong Custer and the Battle of the Little Big Horn, they are:

The ABC's of Custer's Last Stand: Arrogance, Betrayal and Cowardice,
    ISBN 0-912783-38-9, 2004

The Original Handwritten Transcript of the Reno Court of Inquiry,
    ISBN 978-0-615-23576-9, 2008

Custer's First Messenger!? Debunking the Story of Sergeant Daniel A. Kanipe,
    ISBN 978-1-4507-7969-2, 2011